Desert to Destiny: The Daughters of Zelophehad is more than a book about five obscure Hebrew women. Wendy Yapp has produced a remarkable study of the individual's power to eff̶ ̶ ̶ ̶ ̶ ̶he has breathed life into biblical characters a̶n̶ ̶ ̶ ̶ ̶ ̶ ̶us to identify our own struggles and ̶ ̶ ̶ ̶ ̶ ̶ ̶ghly recommend it—it is im̶ ̶ ̶ ̶ ̶ ̶ ̶nd encouraging.

̶ ̶̶ ̶FONTAINE
̶ ̶̶ ̶, SOUTH AFRICA

Through *Desert to Destiny: The ̶ ̶̶ughters of Zelophehad*, Wendy Yapp offers up hope and destiny whatever our name. Regardless of our background, God is building His characteristics into His children. Wendy takes us on an in-depth journey into the lives of five biblical daughters. She inspires her readers to believe that a life of victory is possible regardless of our circumstances.

—DIANA THOMAS
DIANA THOMAS MINISTRIES, AUSTRALIA

Do you know who the daughters of Zelophehad were? Wendy Yapp takes the few statements that are given us in Scripture and with God-given imagination paints the story behind the story. Yes, much of her story is fiction, but it also brings the Bible record vibrantly alive. And her imagination is kept on track by her wide and thoughtful use of God's Word as she explores many themes springing out of the lives of a family of Old Testament disciples. Compassionate, honest and pastoral—and a good read!

—ROSE DOWSETT
AUTHOR AND TEACHER, OMF SCOTLAND

Wendy Yapp is a weaver of words and a student of word meanings. It's through these endeavors that she has taken often overlooked passages and names and forged indelible life applications. From the dusty pages of history, she shines a light on little-known names and draws life lessons from each one that are so real, you feel as though these people were in your own living room sharing their family stories. Like an investigative reporter, the author has brought insights on ancient customs, traditions and everyday life events and applied them to our own personal spiritual journeys.

—DR. GERALD ROBISON
CO-AUTHOR, *CAT AND DOG THEOLOGY*, AND V.P., UNVEILING GLORY

Is this book a story? A devotional? A word study? An anthology? A commentary? A testimony? It is all of these and none of these. For an intriguing and fascinating read, you need look no further than *Desert to Destiny*.

—Dr. Barry Chant
Author, Senior Pastor, Wesley International Congregation
Sydney, Australia

Truth with gentleness that is veiled in a velvet glove. I love it!

—Beth Sadler
Director, Healing Rooms, Yakima, Washington

Before reading *Desert to Destiny*, I did not know who the daughters of Zelophehad were. Taking the few references about them in the Bible, Wendy Yapp has used her God-given imagination to paint the story behind these five women, but this is more than a fictional story. It is in fact a biblical overview in a narrative style. As you read this highly readable and cleverly crafted book, you will understand more deeply the story of God's people in the Bible.

—Dr. Kim Tan
Author and Business Entrepreneur
Chairman, Jubliee Action, U.K.

Speaking as the parents of five daughters (and no sons!) we naturally have identified with Zelophehad since he came to our attention soon after our youngest two girls (non-identical twins) were born in 1985. When we read about the way those five daughters of Zelophehad pressed through for their inheritance, yet submitted to the injunction that they could only marry within the clan, we laid hold of that for our girls too. Basically, we felt that old Z had gotten something right in his parenting and in modeling the life of faith—something we also aspired to!

—Ross and Christine Paterson
Chinese Church Support Ministries, Singapore

A very unique and challenging book that I know the Holy Spirit will use to inspire greater reality and faith.

—George Verwer
Founder, Operation Mobilisation

Having been an intercessor for thirty-seven years, this book deeply stirred my heart. It is for the whole body of Christ, but I, as an intercessor, kept gleaning hidden truths as the stories continued to unfold about these five daughters. Wendy has skillfully woven in the art of storytelling with the history of the written Word of God.

As the five daughters stood before Moses, they asked a deep question, "Why should the name of our father be removed from among his family because he had no son? Give us a possession among our Father's brothers."

Wendy weaves in the feasts of the Lord and leads the reader into deep understanding of the leadership of God and His servant Moses in the fulfilling of God's covenant promises. I highly recommend that you read this book. You will be provoked to faith by five bold courageous women who leave footprints in the desert sand that help us identify more clearly our individual destiny. The closing three chapters are gripping and educational in our daily walk with the Lord.

—BARBARA (BOBBYE) BYERLEY
AUTHOR, *MIRACLES HAPPEN WHEN WOMEN PRAY*
DIRECTOR OF PRAYER, JERICHO CENTER, U.S.A.

Have you ever wondered about the story behind those mysterious names in the Old Testament? The drama just behind the curtains of stories barely told? Wendy takes you there and lifts the curtain, walking you into the scenes played out thousands of years ago. She shows you, your sisters and your daughters what these ancient stories have to help you today—issues that haven't changed all that much over the ages. You're going to love this book.

—JANICE ROGERS
AUTHOR AND FOUNDER
YOUTH WITH A MISSION AUTHORS' TRAINING SCHOOLS

I have no hesitation in recommending this book to every believer. It will stir and encourage; it will teach and bless; it will strengthen and equip; and it will give you sound, tested and proven steps to follow as you journey through the deserts and storms of your own life.

—REV. DR. MARGARET COURT, MBE, PHD, LLD (HON)
SENIOR PASTOR, VICTORY LIFE CENTRE, PERTH, AUSTRALIA
AUTHOR, WINNING FAITH, WINNING WORDS AND OUR WINNING POSITION

DESERT TO DESTINY

THE DAUGHTERS OF ZELOPHEHAD

WENDY YAPP

CREATION
HOUSE PRESS
A STRANG COMPANY

DESERT TO DESTINY: THE DAUGHTERS OF ZELOPHEHAD
by Wendy Yapp
Published by Creation House Press
A Strang Company
600 Rinehart Road
Lake Mary, Florida 32746
www.creationhouse.com

This book or parts thereof may not be reproduced in any form, stored in a retrieval system or transmitted in any form by any means—electronic, mechanical, photocopy, recording or otherwise—without prior written permission of the publisher, except as provided by United States of America copyright law.

Unless otherwise noted, the Scripture quotations are from the New King James Version of the Bible. Copyright © 1979, 1980, 1982 by Thomas Nelson, Inc., publishers. Used by permission.

Scripture quotations marked NLT are from the Holy Bible, New Living Translation, copyright © 1996. Used by permission of Tyndale House Publishers, Inc., Wheaton, IL 60189. All rights reserved.

Scripture quotations marked NIV are from the Holy Bible, New International Version. Copyright © 1973, 1978, 1984, International Bible Society. Used by permission.

Scripture quotations marked NASB are from the New American Standard Bible. Copyright © 1960, 1962, 1963, 1968, 1971, 1972, 1973, 1975, 1977, 1995 by the Lockman Foundation. Used by permission. (www.Lockman.org)

Scripture quotations marked KJV are from the King James Version of the Bible.

Unless otherwise noted, word definitions and derivations are from *Strong's Exhaustive Concordance of the Bible*, ed. James Strong (Nashville, TN: Thomas Nelson Publishers, 1997).

Cover design by Ededron J. Hernandez

Editorial services by Mollymook Manuscripts, P.O. Box 689, Ulladulla, NSW 2539, Australia

Copyright © 2003 by Wendy Yapp

All rights reserved

Library of Congress Catalog Card Number: 2003109766

International Standard Book Number: 1-59185-287-0

03 04 05 06   8 7 6 5 4 3 2 1

Printed in the United States of America

*This book is lovingly dedicated to my wonderful
husband, Kai Seen,
And our precious children,
Shaeron, Kirstine and Jared,
My constant source of joy.*

*I have no greater joy than to hear that
my children are walking in the truth.*
—3 JOHN 4, NIV

ACKNOWLEDGMENTS

Writing this book has been a journey—invigorating at times, frustrating at others, but never lonesome. People have patiently traveled alongside, giving me invaluable support en route. Many played their part years ago by providing equipment for the expedition.

Some ignited in me a passion for the Word of God including Dick and Rose Dowsett, Eric Alexander, Roger Forster, Donald P. McCallum and my lecturers at Glasgow BTI.

Others equipped me by teaching me about intercession: Royston Clarke, now in glory—model pastor, wonderful friend and mighty man of prayer; Lois Allen, who taught me everything she knew about prayer before she too slipped off to heaven; Bobbye Byerly, intercessor extraordinaire, who always offers a listening ear and nuggets of wisdom.

Many cushioned me in prayer when I hit bumps in the

road—especially Charlotte, Christiane, Laurel, Deb, Kim, Jenny, Ruth, Susan, Tina, Vicki, Sherry, Derek and others at KAC—they, and many others, placed an intercessory imprint on every page. I deeply appreciate you all.

Some threw life vests when the journey took me into deep waters I knew little about: Cyril Pritchard gave me lively and invaluable insight into the Greek language; friends and rabbis helped with things Hebrew; Crosswalk.com provided excellent, free study tools; John Blackett answered my many questions, often the same ones over; my Australian editor, Clare Steward of Mollymook Manuscripts, taught me much about the craft of writing and made me look a good deal better in the process. When it comes to birthing books, Clare, you are a strong and excellent midwife.

The friendly staff at Strang helped me negotiate the final stages of the book journey—special thanks to Allen Quain and team. Thanks also to those who took time out of out of their very busy schedules to read and endorse this book.

I am grateful to dear friends and family around the globe who have stuck by me through thick and thin and encouraged me through my desert seasons. Friends, I appreciate your love and healing balm.

Finally, the most significant travel companions in my journey, along with my amazing Lord, are my precious family: no husband could have been more loving or supportive than Kai Seen; Jared, our imaginative son, often squashed onto my knee while I worked, correcting my grammar and offering alternative—often better—words! Son, your smiles brighten my days; our beautiful daughters, Shaeron and Kirstine, read each chapter, or at least pretended to, and said, "Great, Mum" no matter how terrible it was. Girls, you truly are daughters of Zelophehad, and I am proud of you both.

No wife, mother, daughter or friend could be more blessed—I love you all.

CONTENTS

Preface: Footprints in the Sand xii

1 Leaving Goshen. 1

2 Zelophehad 16

3 Korah 34

4 Mahlah. 56

5 Noah. 77

6 Hoglah 100

7 Milcah 121

8 Tirzah. 148

9 Character of a Daughter
  of Zelophehad 167

10 Family Matters 193

11 Taking the New Land 203

12 Passing on the Inheritance 215

PREFACE

Footprints in the Sand

"**P**apa, are we there yet?" Mahlah asked, her little legs tired from the long day's walk.

"Not far now," Zelophehad bluffed, with fatherly expertise. He had no other answer for his child, but it was not because he was lost or afraid to ask for directions. Zelophehad's path was clear: he was following the Cloud. He cast a glance towards the sky, and it did not go unnoticed.

"I wish it would stop, Papa. Make it stop," another sweet voice pleaded, echoing the thoughts in Zelophehad's own mind.

"It will stop when it stops, Noah. Be patient, child. The Lord knows where He is taking us."

"Glad someone does," mumbled Mrs. Zelophehad. It was hard terrain, especially for a woman with child. She turned to catch her husband's eye, stumbling over an unnoticed rock in the process. In spite of her swollen belly, she caught herself before she lost her balance completely. Zelophehad, a little too *late, offered a free hand to steady her, but she had a strong, independent streak and brushed him off.*

"I'm OK!" she grimaced. "I can manage. After all these years, I can handle a few rocks, pregnant or not!" Inwardly, she longed for somewhere to stop to rest her aching legs, but if the children could walk then so could she.

"Papa, will you tell us a story?" asked a third small voice. Little girls' voices echoed all around Zelophehad. "Yes, Papa! Yes!"

"The one about Egypt," Mahlah piped up.

"And the sea, Papa," Noah insisted, pushing her sister out of the way and nearly tripping her mother up again in the process.

"And the songs, Papa," Hoglah added quickly, "sing us the songs!" She burst into song as if to convince him it was a good idea, and spontaneously the others joined in. At the sound of singing, the baby in Zelophehad's arms gurgled and clapped excitedly. Baby Milcah always traveled in royal style and did not yet know what sore feet felt like.

In spite of his own weariness, Zelophehad continued to tell the stories and sing the songs. While he entertained his troop, he was quietly training them to follow in his steps. And by doing so, one family left their footprints in the sand.

Of course, we don't know what stories Zelophehad really told his children, but, in keeping with Hebrew tradition, he would have told them many that helped to shape their lives. Our Father has stories for us, too. Some are set in peaceful gardens, others in stormy waters and a few, like this one, take place in the desert. These are like footprints written in the sand, left for us to learn from. Some, like those of Moses, we cannot miss: they are large and clear. Smaller, lighter footprints, like those of the daughters of Zelophehad, are more easily overlooked. But they are there, tucked away at the end of the Book of Numbers. Come, step into the Bible and meet Zelophehad and his five girls! If you haven't heard of them before, I can promise you an exciting journey. It is a journey from desert to destiny.

It was census time, and Moses and his nephew Eleazar were counting the people. To be precise, they were counting only the men, six hundred thousand of them. When they reached Zelophehad's line, something rather remarkable happened.

> Zelophehad son of Hepher had no sons; he had only daughters, whose names were Mahlah, Noah, Hoglah, Milcah and Tirzah.
>
> —NUMBERS 26:33, NIV

Everyone at the census must have done a double take. Whoa! Did we hear right? Not just one woman sneaking into Male Land but five, and all five from one family!

By Numbers 26, Zelophehad's storytelling days were over, and he was no longer alive, but his daughters quietly appeared for a brief but significant moment.

The Promised Land was now in sight, but Moses had a couple of last-minute jobs to do before the people could take possession of their promise. Apart from some basic training in fighting off the enemy, he had a large parcel of land to slice up so that everyone would have a piece to call his own. They had waited a long time for this moment and had eaten a lot of gritty sand in the process. Forget the sandwiches—it was milk and honey cake time now.

It reminds me of kids at a birthday party eagerly looking at a cake decorated with lots of goodies. Who gets the cherries? Who gets the largest, sweetest slice? A good parent knows it is wise to slice a cake so that everyone gets a fair portion of icing. The people had been promised a sweet reward, but it would not be a "free for all" stampede to get at the goodies. God is a God of order. He knows exactly the portion of land for each person. So after the head count came the land allotment, according to the size of the tribe.

Rebellions and plagues had significantly altered tribe

demographics since the last census, thirty-eight years previously. (See Numbers 1:2.) Simeon had entered the desert the third largest tribe, but left it by far the smallest. Manasseh, the tribe Zelophehad belonged to, had started out as the smallest group, but it showed the most increase in the desert and, by the second census, was one of the largest: it was a blessed tribe.

Now here they were, excited about discovering the extent of their portion. Women, it was assumed, were not allowed a slice of the cake; they had to share with fathers, brothers or husbands and accept this as a fact of life. Except for the daughters of Zelophehad. Let's read what happened when the girls are mentioned for the third time.

> Then came the daughters of Zelophehad... from the families of Manasseh the son of Joseph; and these were the names of his daughters: Mahlah, Noah, Hoglah, Milcah, and Tirzah. And they stood before Moses, before Eleazar the priest, and before the leaders and all the congregation, by the doorway of the tabernacle of meeting, saying: "Our father died in the wilderness; but he was not in the company of those who gathered together against the Lord, in company with Korah, but he died in his own sin; and he had no sons. Why should the name of our father be removed from among his family because he had no son? Give us a possession among our father's brothers." So Moses brought their case before the Lord. And the Lord spoke to Moses, saying: "The daughters of Zelophehad speak what is right; you shall surely give them a possession of inheritance among their father's brothers, and cause the inheritance of their father to pass to them. And you shall speak to the children of Israel, saying: 'If a man dies and has no son, then you shall cause his inheritance to pass to his daughter.'"
> —NUMBERS 27:1–11

I suspect that, long after the daughters were dead and gone, each time this part of the Torah was read, every woman's ears pricked up. These five young women went before the leaders of their day and asked for something no other woman dared to dream of: a slice of the cake! The Lord granted the sisters' request, but, as often happens when changes take place, it caused some concerns in the extended family. (See Numbers 36:1–12.) The third mention of the daughters of Zelophehad deals with these concerns, but the story does not end there.

The women had another important visit to make, this time to Joshua, and for that they had to wait patiently, holding onto their promises, while the battle for the land was won. (See Joshua 17:3–6.)

Compared to men, few women are mentioned throughout biblical history, but the daughters of Zelophehad are recorded in five places, four times by name. Of their contemporaries, only Miriam received more coverage in the Desert Woman's *Who's Who*. She was considered the lone woman of influence in the desert. At least it might seem that way at first.

Are you hungry to take the land of your prophetic promises? Running around in circles in the desert, unable to find your promised living water? Feeling as if you have somehow missed out on your rightful portion because of circumstances, gender or age?

Maybe, just maybe, these women can show us the way. Let's return to the desert, to Zelophehad's story, and examine those footprints a little more carefully...

CHAPTER 1

Leaving Goshen

*Moses and Aaron went in and told Pharaoh,
"Thus says the LORD God of Israel: 'Let My
people go...'"*

—EXODUS 5:1

"Well, my little ones," Zelophehad began, "Papa grew up in a place far away from here."

"Goshen," interrupted Mahlah who, being the eldest, had heard this story many times before.

"Yes, child," Zelophehad affirmed, smiling tenderly, "Goshen Province, in Rameses, a city where Pharaoh kept his vast treasure and supplies. Everything from grain to gold." Zelophehad knew the word gold would capture their imaginations. "The bowls were golden; there were golden thrones and many golden statues." The girls' eyes sparkled at the thought.

"Our forefather Joseph chose Goshen because it was a great place to live. That was in the 'good old days,' but, girls, the good times didn't last for long." Zelophehad drew a deep breath as he recalled some things he would not tell his young daughters yet. Yes, he had been delivered, but the memory of childhood trauma flooded back and made him wince within. He shut his eyes *instinctively, as if by closing them he could close off the pain. Without realizing it, he stopped talking for a brief moment. He had never known Goshen in good days. All he had known was a hard life and a far-off God who allowed His people to suffer. That was until Moses came along, and then the fun began.*

"Go on, Papa," little Mahlah urged, tugging on his sleeve.

So Zelophehad recounted, in a fatherly manner, the hard days in Goshen and the happier days when deliverance came. His daughters soon forgot their weariness and managed to trudge an extra few miles of their journey that day.

GOSHEN, A GOOD PLACE

Goshen contained the best land in Egypt. Joseph gave his brothers the *best part of the land* to settle in, and the *fat of the land* to eat. (See Genesis 45:18; 47:11.) Fat, in the Bible, refers to the sweetest and best part, and Goshen was sweet compared to the rest of Egypt, which was dry and barren. This easterly part was on the fertile flood plains.

Goshen means "rain," an appropriate name for the area with the highest rainfall in the region.[1] For Jacob's refugee family, who were shepherds, this was prime grazing country, an excellent location. In Egypt theirs was a lowly job, but Joseph's brothers immediately soared within the pastoral ranks to become the Pharaoh's shepherds. Goshen, for Jacob & Sons, became a land of provision, positioning and promotion, just as it had been for Joseph before their arrival.

It was a hub of activity and prosperity with: "canals full of fish, lakes swarming with birds, fields of lentils, melons, wheat, onions and sesame, gardens of vines, almonds and figs. Ships entered its harbor; the lotus and papyrus grew in its waters."[2]

Goshen was a place of prolific multiplication and growth—not just of produce and trade. Jacob's family grew to such an extent that they became a headache for pharaohs to come.

But Goshen was more than just good pastureland and

abundance of every kind. Its name also means "drawing near," and that is what happened with Joseph and his estranged brothers. Forgiveness was extended and received in Goshen, and broken relationships were restored.

OUR GOSHENS

It does sound like a great spot, doesn't it? Many of us have been, metaphorically, to Goshen. If we look back on our lives, we can see places where the Lord has taken us after seasons of spiritual famine. In the early days they were, for us, places of growth and favor, positioning and promotion, restoration and reconciliation.

Looking back on our Goshens will bring floods of happy memories. Those were the days! The fellowship was great, and the food was fantastic, making famine pale in our memories. Goshen was the best! It was indeed a choice place to be—at least for a while.

GOSHEN: CRUMBLING STATUES AND STATUTES

After Joseph's death, Goshen changed and was never the same again. New anti-Semitic pharaohs came to power and, unsympathetic to the growing band of shepherds, turned them into slaves. Over the years, the Egyptians tore down the statues of Joseph, and the statutes of freedom and favor were no longer valid. Shepherds' crooks were exchanged for bricks, and the Hebrews were forced to build the twin cities of Rameses and Pithom.

RAMESES, CITY OF FALSE GODS

Place names often tell us something of the history of a place. I was brought up in the Scottish village of Balfron, "village of mourning." Legend has it that wolves came down from the hills and devoured village children, leaving a community in grief. The school coat of arms bore wolf and hills, a gory reminder for us kids not to venture too far, although the wolves had been long gone. Rameses and Pithom also have interesting name meanings.

Rameses, after Pharaoh's son of the same name, means "son of the sun god."[3] It is ironic and rather sad that the sons of God built the "son of the sun god" city. The Lord had plans for them to build a city that could not be shaken, and here they were, busy building an idolatrous metropolis that was destined to fall!

Rameses was a store city; it housed Pharaoh's treasures and grain. Can you imagine building a granary but not being able to eat the grain?

That's what was happening to the Hebrews. While Pharaoh satisfied his lust for power and filled his belly with choice grain, the Hebrew brickmakers had to slave for every kernel to feed their families. That is what empire building did—and still does. A few people ate well, but most, stuck with only stalks to make bricks, remained hungry.

There was another hunger building in the people: a hunger for deliverance. They were sick of living in a city named after both a cruel pharaoh and a false god.

Not all the Hebrews were brickmakers; some had the task of making idols. Although they were poor slaves, these men handled Pharaoh's gold and crafted it into dazzling creations. Their skill later caused trouble when they made the golden calf, but it also prepared artisans able to make beautiful items for the tabernacle. Rameses, for all its idolatry, had taught the Hebrews something that would later be used for God's glory.

Pithom, City of Justice

Pithom was another treasure storage center with an interesting name meaning "City of Justice." It did not live up to the name. Pithom, for the Hebrews, was a place of injustice and hardship. Imagine being ordered to build a city called "Justice" when everything around was screaming, "It's not fair! Injustice!" I wonder if Zelophehad ever cried out, "How long, O Lord? How long!"

Another meaning of *Pithom* is "mouthful."[4] I am sure, after four hundred and thirty years, the Hebrews had had a mouthful of Pithom, with its bitter taste of slavery.

The third meaning for *Pithom* is "house of Tum," Tum being another sun god.[5] So *Pithom* implies "the house of a god." Once again, it is one destined to perish.

LESSONS IN PITHOM

Injustice will come to us all, especially to those who have chosen to pick up their cross and follow Jesus. He was the epitome of everything just, but He suffered the greatest injustices of all time. If we are truly following Jesus, injustices will at some point tag along on our tails, and we must take them to the cross and place them at His feet. Many rich lessons are learned in Injustice City. Once we have tasted its bitterness, we learn to deal more graciously with others. We know its pain and do not want others to suffer it.

Injustice makes us hungry for justice and vindication. It makes us scream inside for the Lord to show us as blameless in a situation and to restore the honor of our name. But God's justice without His mercy is an impossible thing for any man to bear, without Christ in the picture. We would be better off leaving the vindication in the Lord's hands and asking Him to pour out His mercy upon those who have wounded, grieved or insulted us. Forgiveness, that very thing which releases us from the pain of the situation, will come much easier to our hearts when we pray for God's mercy and leave the timing, if ever, of any vindication with Him.

The lessons of Pithom are hard to see when the pain of injustice is intense, but they are there, and one day they will be weaved into our future and into our ability to take our inheritance. Had the Hebrews never tasted injustice, they would have carried on living peacefully in Goshen, accepting Pharaoh's best choice, but unaware that the Lord had much more for them. The injustice spurred intercession and carried with it important lessons. Each brick laid in injustice built the muscles that would later build a nation. For us, our reactions to the trials we face determine how effectively we will build in the future. Learning to deal with injustice is like a stamp on our passports to fulfilling our destiny. One day we will be glad that stamp is there.

I had a time when I was treated very unfairly. The situation had a profound impact on our whole family and caused us terrible pain. It was a battle to forgive and to move on. It became a case of "Eyes forward, soldier, march on." Some days that was so hard to do I could barely stand up, never mind march, and my prayer life was reduced to groans. It was a time of intense tears and anguish, and some days the injustice of it seemed more than I could bear. Then, very gently, the Lord gave me a few strategies to help me focus: He sent one from halfway around the world.

A woman in the U.S., whom I barely knew, sent me a message tape about how tough times train us to be "carriers of God's glory."[6] Over and over again, when the pain and injustice of the situation rose in my heart, I listened to the tape. Slowly, my pain was soothed, hope rose in my heart and forgiveness was released. Wounded people need simple strategies, and this one was simple: focus on the Lord by listening to His Word.

The Lord might not send you an anointed tape from a stranger half a world away, but He will have a strategy for you to help you get through your Pithom.

DELIVERANCE IN GOSHEN

> Now it came about in the course of those many days that the king of Egypt died. And the sons of Israel *sighed* because of the bondage, and they *cried out*, and their *cry*

for help because of their bondage rose up to God.
—EXODUS 2:23, NASB, EMPHASIS ADDED

Three words give us insight into how the Hebrews cried out to God, each word building on the next:

1. *Sighed* means "groaned in pain, gasped and moaned like cattle."

This cry is personal and often expressed privately. Intercessors will know this kind of travail, like a woman in birth, groaning over Goshen situations affecting individuals, churches, cities and even nations.

I heard this moan in a hospital in Borneo where I was giving birth to our daughters. As an expatriate, I had the privilege of a private room, but for most of the patients, there was very little privacy until the last stage of labor. Moans and cries seemed to come from all parts of the room, and I understood why someone might say women in labor sound like cattle. Many in the room were the wives of Ghurkha soldiers I taught English to, but the women themselves spoke little English or the local language, Malay. Expressions of agony, however, need little interpretation the world over.

2. *Cried out* means "called to one's aid in a time of need."

Elsewhere this word is translated "joined together" and "proclamation." It is a corporate calling, a summoning of the Lord together. Extreme pressure, as it often does, brought people together in prayer.

3. *Cry* is "a loud cry or shout."

This cry turns the volume up even more and is a sign of desperate, fervent, often corporate prayer. David knew this cry: "In my distress I called upon the LORD, and cried out to my God; He heard my voice from His temple, and my *cry* came before Him, even to His ears" (Ps. 18:6, emphasis added).

These are the cries that open God's ears. When a community is mourning and crying out to the Lord together for release from the enemy's rule, then God shows up and brings deliverance and societal change.

It was not the pressures in Goshen that made the Lord's hand move, or because Pharaoh had a change of heart and decided to let them go. Neither were they delivered because a mighty person with great charisma rose up to lead them. They were delivered because they cried out together for help, and those *cries* reached heaven's ears: "I have heard their cries for deliverance" (Exod. 3:7, NLT, emphasis added).

From the Hebrew perspective, nothing had changed. If God had heard their cries for community transformation, it didn't look like it! What had their cries accomplished? They were still making bricks and being beaten. But God was getting the answering process quietly under way on a mountain far from Goshen. The prayers in Goshen were fueling a fire that would later set a nation ablaze, deliver it and set it free.

While the Hebrews were on their knees, a prince-turned-shepherd encountered God in the burning bush. Moses had been contentedly minding his own business, sheep, but suddenly found he had to go on a mission for God's flocks. Those on the plains of Goshen had to wait until Moses came down the mountain, sorted out his business and took a long walk to Egypt. In the meantime, the desperate Hebrews cried out for help, day after day, little knowing it was already on its way.

ON THE MOVE AGAIN

We as a family have had many occasions when the Lord has sent the answer even before we have said "amen" to our prayers. One occasion was when we were praying about moving, yet again. The Lord had been challenging us about our call to missions, but since my husband's call is tied up with his work as an engineer, we needed to be in a country where he was able to get a job. We talked and prayed over the issue for many months but were unsure about moving our children once more. One weekend, while praying with friends about our concerns, we sensed the Lord calling us to move to Australia, and, in spite of our hesitations, we were willing to obey.

Less than two days later, the phone rang with an unexpected permanent job offer in Australia. The procedures for that offer were well under way before we prayed. God was ahead of us, having heard our previous cries, but He waited until we had grasped the Australia factor and expressed our willingness to obey before He released the answer. Within two months, Kai Seen was in Australia, and our family was in transition once more.

Days of Transition

Before long, Moses was in Goshen. Soon after his arrival, some interesting and unusual things happened. Zelophehad and the others had longed for a leader like Moses to arise and set them free, but they had not expected things to get quite as messy. The pressure of slavery was one thing, and they had been used to that, but the pressure of pending freedom was a new experience.

Egypt's irrigation system was useless because of dead fish and blood-tainted water. The Egyptians could not drink the water, clothes could not be washed and the place stank of rotten fish. Then came the frogs.

I have not experienced a frog plague, but I have been through a millipede invasion. We were on vacation, and one evening, it seemed as if every millipede in the land was crawling into our cottage. Every hour we swept up hundreds into a dustpan and threw them as far away as possible. Being a zoologist who dislikes insects, I devised scientific ways to keep the creatures out of the house, but still millions of marching little legs made their way over the floor and up the walls. At least millipedes are not slimy and do not croak. Can you imagine a carpet of croaking frogs while you are trying to sleep? And what would it be like if you had to get up in the night to relieve yourself?

Zelophehad's dreams were becoming confused. He expected deliverance to look and feel a lot better than this. When he went to work in the Egyptian areas, there were flies and frogs everywhere, the Egyptians had nasty boils they wanted the servants to dress and several times he had to dash for cover when giant hailstones fell. He knew things were changing, and for a while Zelophehad didn't know if he was coming or going. Still, faith was building in his heart: there were no flies, disease or boils in the Hebrew townships.

This choicest land was no longer choice; it was a bloodied, stinking, awful place, but the word on the grapevine was that God's people were leaving—soon. News of pending deliverance spread like wildfire through the oppressed community and reached Zelophehad's ears.

"Did you hear what Moses did today?"

"Did you hear what he is up to now?"

"Are you with him or not?"

"Are you coming or not?"

GOSHEN GRAPEVINES

Goshen had an effective grapevine. For two million people to get themselves together and on the move so fast, it had to be good. How the grapevine operated determined, at least in part, the people's ability to move into their inheritance. It was both an asset and a liability. As a positive quality, it helped the Hebrews out of bondage, but later it came into negative use and kept a generation in the desert.

All of our churches have grapevines. It is part of human nature, part of connecting with one another, so we must make sure we use it wisely. Grapevines are great if they are producing fruitful talk that is wholesome, strengthening and edifying. Women, who tend to talk more to one another than men, should be particularly responsible. The church's grapevine should be laden with gracious speech rather than complaints or gossip. How much better to have a grapevine bursting with the Word of God and testimonies of the wonderful things He is doing around the world in our day! When we hear this kind of talk on the grapevine, it builds faith and liberates the men as well as the women.

LEAVING GOSHEN BEHIND

Rameses was pregnant and swollen to birthing point with God's chosen people, including Zelophehad and his wife. One of the largest moves of people in history was about to take place, and Zelophehad, along with two million others, was to be a part of it. Two million people! That's a lot of people to get from Brickland to Sandyland in a few small maneuvers. Pharaoh's reluctance to let God's people go was understandable: his whole economy was on the line. How can you replace a million brickmakers and field hands? It was perhaps the biggest industrial walkout of all time.

> The Israelites set out from Rameses on the fifteenth day of the first month, the day after Passover. They marched out boldly and in full view of all the Egyptians, who were burying all their firstborn.
> —NUMBERS 33:3, NIV

Can you imagine what a family snapshot of this event would look like? Those who were once the captors were now stunned, their faces locked behind bars of disbelief and grief. Those who were once slaves were now bold, radiating the glow of freedom. *Boldly* here means "to rise up and be exalted." Some translations use "bold defiance" or "with a high hand."[7] It must have been the biggest "give me five, brother" of all time.

There was a measure of defiance in the way the Israelites moved out. Not all defiance is bad: we are allowed to defy the enemy. A good defiance stares into the enemy's face and says, "I want my inheritance, and I am leaving the things that have enslaved me so that I can get it!" Moses, Aaron, Zelophehad and the masses were standing tall as they stared into the enemy's face, and he could do nothing about it.

Liberation does that to us. It enables us to stand tall and be able to see situations from a different perspective.

I once noticed a young man at Lee Abbey, a Christian community in England. He walked in a strange manner, chin high in the air, yet still able to see straight before him. I was intrigued by his posture and so was delighted when he told me his story. At one time he could not look people in the eye and always walked with his head down. Then he met Jesus, and the Lord instructed him to lift his chin and walk tall: this had changed his outlook on life entirely.

So how do we know when we are in a Goshen situation that we must move on from? Our salvation experience, of course, is our first Goshen. Our lives before accepting Christ may have seemed choice and easy places to be, until the slavery to sin was exposed. But there are other Goshen times, harder to identify and often more easily seen in retrospect. Looking back, we may remember a situation where we felt like an eaglet in a comfy nest, learning, growing and fluttering our wings. But then, just as a father eagle would do for his young, the Lord allowed our soft nest to be stirred up and become uncomfortable, leaving us with no choice but to get out, stretch our wings and fly.

Of course, that does not mean every hard place is a Goshen

we must leave. Tough times will come and go, leaving lessons in their wake for those who endure. Having said that, there are times when, in order to move us forward into our call, the Lord will stir up our nests and move us onto the next stop.

FIRST STOP SUCCOTH

So Zelophehad and his young wife, with great joy and excitement, found their place in the mighty train of people heading towards the Red Sea. They had never been out of Goshen before, and each new step filled them with exhilaration. Zelophehad noticed old women, normally bent over, with a spring in their step. His wife was observing the children who were dancing along gaily and chirping happily with each other. In spite of the energy in the air, the people eventually needed a rest. Their first stop was at Succoth.

Two Succoths are mentioned in the Bible: this one and a place where Jacob stopped to rest his cattle. (See Exodus 12:37; Genesis 33:17.) Both Succoth stops were resting points for the people and animals after a lengthy walk. Succoth means "cattle booth" or "temporary shelter." It can also be translated "tabernacle," and, as we shall see later, this stop is commemorated in one of the Jewish feasts, the Feast of Tabernacles. Pithom, house of a false god, was not the home the Lord wanted for His people or for Himself. He had a living tabernacle in mind.

Jacob, like the Hebrews, had left a place of bondage under his father-in-law, Laban. He had crossed a few treacherous rivers, the Euphrates ("place of breaking") and the Jabbok ("place of emptying") and had experienced a struggle with God that left him with a limp and a name change. He then moved into a period of R and R—rest and reconciliation—reconciling with Esau, then stopping for a rest at Succoth.

Succoth was the stop the Hebrews needed for refreshment after their ordeal in captivity. For them it was indeed a time of great rejoicing, allowing the events of the past few days to sink in: they were free! Today, amongst the feasts, it is acknowledged as the happiest of all.

Succoths are significant for us in our journey, too. Just as the Lord provided rest for His people at Succoth, our Father has a resting place for us after times of hard work, stress and spiritual battle. When we leave a Goshen behind us, we should find this place to rest and, if necessary, seek reconciliation with estranged brothers or sisters in Christ before moving onto the next stage of our journey.

JESUS' SUCCOTH

Before leaving this stop, there is one more type of Succoth we should look at; I call it "Jesus' Succoth." Jesus was born, many believe, during the Feast of Tabernacles, in a cattle booth, fulfilling the prophetic pictures of Succoth. It is as if heaven was shouting, "God wants to tabernacle with mankind!" in every way possible.

> The Word became flesh and dwelt [or tabernacled] among us.
> —JOHN 1:14, NASB

But Jesus was not leaving a Goshen; He was coming so that we could leave ours.

God was telling His children, "The first stop will be a temporary shelter, so don't get too settled there."

Succoth also means "thicket," and we all know that Abraham found his sacrificial lamb in a thicket. So do we. The Lord is the sacrificial lamb, in the tabernacle, in the cattle shed. He fulfilled all three meanings in one push from Mary's womb!

Succoth for us is a joyful rest stop, but not for long. We need wisdom and obedience to take our rest stops and to revel in joy. But we also need to hear when He says, "Time to move on!"

Zelophehad, being an ordinary man, probably couldn't guess how prophetically rich Succoth was, but he would have told his girls what he knew. Their journey that day was nearly over when he told them about seas parting, charioteers drowning and the sheer euphoria of reaching the other side. As he tucked his tired children into bed that night, Zelophehad sang to them Miriam's song of deliverance.

He had talked his little ones through many a day's walk. His stories kept them moving and reminded Zelophehad himself why he was walking around in the desert. Storytelling brought back memories of the stories his own dad had told him. As he bedded down that night, he smiled as he thought about his own favorite, "The Family Tree." The camp was quiet, but as Zelophehad drifted off to sleep, he was remembering sights and sounds of days long gone by—days of slavery.

CHAPTER 2

Zelophehad

*…Zelophehad the son of Hepher, the son of
Gilead, the son of Machir, the son of Manasseh.*
—NUMBERS 27:1

"**P**apa," *quizzed young Zelophehad as he molded some
straw and mud together, "doesn't Pharaoh ever get tired
of bricks?" Hepher laughed heartily. "Not so far, son, but one
day, one day." Hepher took the half-molded brick and finished
it properly. No one would beat his son for making a bad brick
today or any day while he was still around.*

*As soon as Zelo's tiny hands were able, the Egyptians had
put him to work. Hepher kept a watchful eye on his son, and if
the boy tired or became distracted, he whispered, "Keep going,
son." When the taskmasters were not listening, Hepher encouraged the lad with stories from long ago, the same stories that
Zelo would later share with his own troop in the desert.*

Zelo's favorite was "The Family Tree."

*"Son," Hepher began, knowing his son enjoyed this story,
"tell what your name means."*

"Shadow and fear, Papa."

16

ZELOPHEHAD

"And why did we call you that?" Zelophehad glanced up from his brickmaking and pointed his chin towards the Egyptian taskmasters. His father nodded, but there were other reasons too. *"It all started in Eden …"*

Hepher went on to describe the breakdown in relationship between God and man when Adam sinned. Cleverly, he weaved the themes contained in Zelophehad's name through his story.

"Adam was so scared," Hepher continued, *"he ran to the shadows and hid in fear."* Zelophehad knew the story inside out, but never tired of hearing it yet again. After Adam, Hepher moved on to Cain and Abel and highlighted the fear and dark shadows that murder and jealousy had caused. Hepher was a skillful storyteller who brought history alive for his son. He told the stories of Noah, a man who feared the Lord and saw the shadows of storm clouds being cast on the ground long before the rains fell, Abraham, who was not afraid to obey the Lord, and Isaac, Jacob, Joseph and his sons. Each had their shadows and each their fears.

All the Hebrews could trace their roots to Jacob, but not all to the great respected leader Joseph, once prime minister of the world's strongest power. Joseph had been a rags-to-riches, pit-to-pyramid kind of guy. Zelophehad was proud to have Joseph's blood in his veins and share the same family tree. Father and son labored steadily for the rest of the day, and Hepher's stories lightened their load, making the hours seem shorter.

The sun was setting, and the great pyramids cast giant shadows onto the land, as if on cue. Their quota of bricks was now complete, and the pair, tired and weary from a day's work, started towards home. By the time they reached their simple dwelling, Hepher had exhausted every fear and shadow, good or bad, that he could think of and touched on most parts of their family tree. They sat down together on the doorstep and dusted the sand from swollen feet with their hands.

"So that's your name, my boy!" Hepher clapped his hands together causing the dust to fly off like a puff of smoke. *"Now, let's put it on the family tree."*

He picked up a stick that was lying within reach and drew a simple tree in the sand. Zelophehad crouched down to see more clearly. Dusk was well underway, and the shadows were giving way to darkness, but Zelophehad could still see his name at the top of the tree.

"Don't let any shadow or fear ever hold you down, my son!" Zelophehad did not hear; he was absorbed in trying to write his name in the sand with his finger. Hepher chortled at his attempt then, taking the boy by the hand. He pulled him up, and together they went to eat.

What's in a Name?

Not all names carry significance, but many do, especially Hebrew ones. Adam (man), Jesus (Savior), Job (hated or persecuted one), Ruth (friend), Samuel (heard of God). The list could fill a book; in fact, the Word of God abounds with people whose names speak of their past or point prophetically to their future. For many, the Lord changed their names when they moved into a new stage of their personal destiny. Abram became Abraham, Jacob became Israel, Gideon became Jerubbaal and Saul became Paul.

The Chinese also take names seriously. My husband's name, Kai Seen, suits him well: Kai meaning "integrity" and Seen, "faith." Chinese people do not need to look up baby name books to discover the meanings of their names—they are obvious and are a frequent topic of conversation.

With Western names we sometimes need a little creative license, which prophetic people love to use! My name is a good example. *Wendy Jane* means both the "friendly, wandering grace of God" and "fair one with grace." The first meaning is apt since, by God's grace, I have wandered around the globe a fair bit. I love the second meaning more, however, because it means there is a Bible verse written with my name all over it, "Rise up, my love, my fair one, and come away" (Song of Sol. 2:10)!

Names should be a blessing, but sometimes, no matter how creatively we look at them, they carry a sting. But there is hope! Remember Jabez, whose name means "pain"? Bruce Wilkinson highlighted this name in his book, The *Prayer of Jabez*, and shows how even a "painful" name can be transformed to become a prayer of blessing.[1] Perhaps you need to do a "Jabez" and ask the Lord for the flip side of the coin. And remember, when flipping your coin, you are the head and not the tail! (See Deuteronomy 28:13, 44.)

It is not just first names that bear significance. The middle or family name can be just as significant, and sometimes the blessing of a "stinging" first name is seen only in the context of the other given names.

Once I was discussing names with a group of girls from Youth With a Mission. The girls were all chatting excitedly about what their names meant. One young Canadian with quiet embarrassment told us that her name, Leah, meant "weak eyes." Surely the Lord didn't want her to have weak sight! We ran a search on the computer to see if what she had been told was correct. We discovered that the biblical Leah indeed had weak eyes, but her name actually meant "weary." At that, Leah's face fell even further. I asked if she had a middle name, and when she told me it was Shiloh, I nearly hit the roof with excitement. I knew she was in for a treat.

Shiloh was a well-known biblical city where the tabernacle was placed. It speaks of God's presence with His people and means "peace, rest and prosperity." It is also considered a name of Jesus.[2] A relieved and teary-eyed Leah Shiloh realized her name meant "rest, peace and prosperity for the weary." In the end, it turned out to be a name that bore a prophetic message for her life, and it suits her well.

If meanings of names weren't important to you when you named your child, and you now find they have unpleasant meanings, then you can always give them a nickname with special significance.

Some people have heard the Lord call them by a special name or title, used affectionately and only by Him. He may call you "Warrior Woman" or "Gentle Man" or perhaps "My Precious Child." It will suit you to a tee, or simply let you know His love more. One thing is for sure, your name may never be world famous, but it is written on the palm of God's hand.

ZELOPHEHAD

As far as we know, Zelophehad was not famous in his day. He was not a priest or a prince and was not prominent, although traditionally he is regarded as a Tsedik or righteous man. We know only a few things about him. Zelophehad:

- was from the smallest tribe, Manasseh.

- was born in Egypt.

- lived a young life of slavery and experienced the plagues and the Exodus.

- went through the "Red Sea Rumble," experienced the "Desert Grumble" and most of the dramatic events of the Books of Exodus and Numbers.

- was not a part of the rebellion led by the priest Korah (we will look at Korah in the next chapter), and his death was not linked in any way to that rebellion.

- had no sons to inherit his land.

- produced five brave daughters.

> A cloud came and overshadowed them; and they were
> fearful as they entered the cloud.
>
> —LUKE 9:34

How do we know when we being overshadowed by the Cloud? A good indicator is how much fear of the Lord is in our hearts. I wonder if Zelophehad, our shadow-fear man, ever made that connection?

The Cloud is just one word picture the Lord uses to demonstrate His shade. He also describes it in terms of the shadow of His wings and the shade of a tree.

God describes Himself as having wings. The Holy Spirit, as a dove, brooded over creation, extending His wings over the earth and making it bear fruit. God's wings are always fruitful wherever they hover and cast their shadow. They are a place of brooding where darkness is transformed to light.

His wings, like His Cloud, cover, protect and provide shade for us. They shield us from marauding foxes and wolves in sheep's clothing that would try to devour His children.

> O Jerusalem...how often I have longed to gather your
> children together, as a hen gathers her chicks under
> her wings, but you were not willing.
>
> —MATTHEW 23:37, NIV

The Lord does not force His wings over us, but beckons to us as he extends them—all we have to do is to be willing to come under.

How many of us have suffered at some time from the same reticence as Jerusalem? I wonder how many times the Lord has said over our lives, "Oh, _(insert your name)_ . How often I have longed to gather you under my wings, but you were not willing!" We fight, struggle and wait until things are too hot to handle before we finally give up our own fight and race under His protective wings. But God does not want His wings used for emergencies only; He wants us to live there.

> He who dwells in the shelter of the Most High will rest in the shadow of the Almighty...He will cover you with His feathers, and under His wings you will find refuge...you will not fear.
>
> —PSALM 91:1, 4–5, NIV

What a list of blessings for heavenly wing dwellers: rest for those who are tired, refuge for those who are being besieged, covering for those who are naked, and no fear.

This verse links the themes of fear and shadow found in Zelophehad's name. If we step out of His shadow, we have every reason to be afraid. But if we stay close to the Good Shepherd, even the valley of death, Satan's terror-filled counterfeit shadow, can be walked through without fear. (See Psalm 23.) Two shadows and two fears: one dark and foreboding, the other a protective place of comfort. If we choose wisely, then we have no need to fear—and every reason to sing!

SINGING, CLINGING, WINGING

> I sing in the shadow of your wings. My soul clings to you.
>
> —PSALM 63:7–8, NIV

I call this the "Singing, Clinging, Winging Verse." When we cling to His wings, we can sing in the darkest of nights and in the driest desert times. It makes me think not only of Paul and Silas in prison singing their hearts out, but also of modern day believers who have faced imprisonment with a song. (See Acts 16:25.)

A friend of mine, a mother of small children, was jailed in a Muslim country because of her faith. I asked how she got through such a dangerous time. "We fasted," she answered simply, "and we sang."

Another lady I know, Diana Thomas, was one of eight expatriate Christians imprisoned in Afghanistan by the Taliban regime. Diana told me how important worship was to them during their ordeal. They sang heartily each day; many new songs were birthed in those Afghan prisons, including one based on Psalm 16:5–6: "Lord, you have assigned me my portion and my cup; you have made my lot secure. The boundary lines have fallen for me in pleasant places; surely I have a delightful inheritance" (NIV).

How can an Afghan prison be pleasant, secure and delightful? Diana said although there were many scary moments, it was spiritually one of the best times in her life. Not only that, Diana told me how she heard how their worship had impacted a prison guard. She said:

> I recently heard of a Pakistani pastor who had been visited by a man asking to know more about Jesus. The pastor asked him where he had heard about Jesus. The man replied, "I served as a prison guard for the Taliban in Afghanistan. I was one of the guards for the American, German and Australian women who were detained by the Taliban. I used to stand outside their cell and listen to them sing and worship Jesus. I often wondered what kind of God could cause these women to worship Him under these conditions. I know I wanted to learn more about Him."

We may not be in prisons like these two ladies, but there are prisons within that can hold us back from our "delightful inheritance." When we push ourselves to sing in tough times, chains of apathy fall off, doors fling open and even if our outer circumstances have not changed, inwardly we enjoy new freedom. Can we always, even when life is at its hardest, sing and cling to His wings?

RUTH AND GOD'S WINGS

Ruth was a woman who did just that. She had suffered many major stress factors in a short space of time including loss of husband and home, culture shock and an international move. She left her own family behind and had an aging mother-in-law to care for. Ruth had every reason to be stressed, but instead she came under the shadow of the Lord's wings and was blessed.

> May the LORD reward your work...the God of Israel, under whose wings you have come to take refuge.
> —RUTH 2:12, NASB

Boaz welcomed Ruth, blessing her decision to find refuge in the Lord; she was not hiding under her mother-in-law's wings, or even initially Boaz's, but under God's. When stressful times hit us, mentors, mother-in-laws and rich relations might be helpful, but our first port of call should always be the Lord.

The word *wings, kanaph,* can also be translated "hidden from view." Our desert seasons are often a time of "being hidden." We are often thrust into those times by misunderstanding, accusation and rejection. Hidden in this way, we find comfort in divine feathers, and our secret teary prayers fill heaven's bowl. Slowly and almost unnoticed, God works in our hearts. We are shoved into these tough times feeling as if we are going into a dark cave, overwhelmed by the prince of darkness. As we come under God's wings, His light starts to shine on us, and the dark cave becomes a light and bright place to be, where the enemy cannot linger.

Kanaph can also be translated "corner of a garment," which takes us back to Ruth. Ruth asks Boaz, as her nearest kinsman, to spread the corner of his garment over her. In doing this, she is asking Boaz to marry her and bring her into an intimate relationship.

Jesus is our Kinsman Redeemer, and He desires us to be His bride. This intimate relationship happens when we ask Him to spread His garment, or His wings, over us. "The ostriches' wings flap joyously with the pinion and plumage of love" (Job 39:13, NAS). Now if an ostrich is likened to having feathers and wings of love, how much more so the

Lord—what a lovely place in which to snuggle up in an attitude of childlike trust!

SHADOWS AND WINGS THAT HEAL

For you who fear My name the sun of righteousness
will rise with healing in its wings.
—MALACHI 4:2, NASB

Healing takes place when we live in the shadow of His wings. In our times of hiddenness, we are healed of our pain and sicknesses and the wounds of the situations that throw us into our deserts. But we do not stay hidden forever. When He is ready, the Son of Righteousness rises, lifting His wings up so that His "chicks" can return to the fields in safety. His wings were wrapped tightly around us, but now, the healing done, He releases us and hovers over us. His wings are outstretched, as in creation. Just as He overshadowed Mary to impregnate her with her destiny, so He overshadows us to impregnate us with our destinies. Underneath His wings, our desert has been turned into destiny. But take heed! This only happens if we are willing to come under the shadow of His wings in the first place!

We do not come out cowering and insecure; when God arises His enemies are scattered. (See Psalm 68:1.) Malachi tells us that we will go out like joyful skipping calves! Our tiredness will melt away, and we will be energetic, anointed and appointed, full of joy and ready to "go into all the world."

And there is more. We come out with wings! Remember, those who wait on the Lord walk, run and soar? (See Isaiah 40:31.) To soar we need wings. When we come under the Lord's wings, we sprout wings so that when He releases us it is as fledglings, with wings that fly and in turn cast shadows that are fruitful.

FRUITFUL SHADOWS

Peter had a fruitful shadow. People who walked in his shadow were healed of their diseases and set free from tormenting spirits. (See Acts 5:15.)

Maria Woodworth Etter, grandmother of the nineteenth century Pentecostal movement, had a powerful shadow, too.

> Signs and wonders too numerous to mention followed her [Maria's] preaching of the Word. It was reported that at some meetings people up to fifty miles away would fall under the power of God and lie for hours. When they eventually were able to get up, they were gloriously saved and often baptized in the Holy Ghost as well.[3]

That is a wide shadow this lady cast over her land!

We cast our shadow too onto other people's lives. If we are gloomy and depressed, our shadows will be of the darker kind and affect people adversely. We will leave them feeling drained, their energies spent on trying to brighten our day. If we have spent time in God's shadow, they will go away changed, encouraged, healed and set free. Chats over coffee or in the marketplace become gentle shadow moments where needy or tired hearts come and sit in the shade of what the Lord has spoken to us. Can you imagine what a billion believers with anointed shadows could do?

ANOTHER FAMILY TREE STORY

Another picture the Lord gives us of His shade is a tree:

> Like an apple tree among the trees of the forest is my lover among the young men. I delight to sit in his shade, and his fruit is sweet to my taste.
> —SONG OF SONGS 2:3, NIV

The symbolism is the same. The Lord is our apple tree, our tree of life, and the fruit is His love that refreshes our souls and renews our strength. He is our delight! The Garden of Eden was created to be a place of enjoyment. (*Eden* means "pleasure and delight.") When we sit contentedly in the Lord's shade, we return to that place of restored relationship and pleasure. We lean on Him, quietly resting our heads on His breast as the disciple John did and connecting to His heartbeat.

This is not the sort of quiet time we snatch whilst driving to work in busy traffic—we can indeed meet God there, but He wants more of us than that. It is not reading the Word, trying to cram in information—that is sitting under the Tree of Knowledge, and although it might feed our minds, it leaves us still feeling hungry deep inside.

The purpose of the Tree of Life is quite different. To sit under this tree takes time. When we linger in its shade and munch on its fruit, we receive mercy, love, grace, freedom and joy. No wonder it is called the Tree of Life. Once we have tasted its fruit, nothing else will satisfy, and we know we have to get to it as often as we can.

Clouds, wings or trees, it doesn't matter which picture you prefer. Under God's shade is a great place to be.

FEAR AND AWE

The second part of Zelophehad's name, *pachad*, means "fear." Today we might call him Zelo Jello! His generation lived under a shadow of fear for many years: fear of not making enough bricks, fear of the oppression they were under, fear of death. Bondage breeds fear—the two go hand in hand.

Pachad is used in many ways throughout Scripture, for both healthy and unhealthy fears.

UNHEALTHY FEAR

Have you ever experienced the crippling effects of fear? All of us have been frozen by its power to some extent or other.

Whether it hits us as fret, worry, indecision, panic or anxiety, they are all unhealthy or ungodly fears. It is a bondage that can be hard to break, but God did it for the Hebrews, and He can do it for us. As then, it still requires our cooperation and faith.

It is strange, sometimes, the things we grow to be afraid of. I was afraid of spiders, moths and flying insects as a child. How I ever decided to study zoology is still a mystery to me! Head knowledge and endless experiments did little to allay my fears. My university colleagues will tell you how I wheeled and dealed my way out of many a collection or dissection because I didn't want to touch "creepy crawlies." It took life in the Tropics to make me face up to these small, but irrational, fears.

However, the biggest fear I have struggled with was connected to spiritual warfare. The last thing I wanted to do was to be involved in serious intercession. It seemed that every time I tried to move forward in this area, I was hit hard: crises would come—car accidents or scares with the children. Slowly and quietly, fear began to take hold of me. I avoided seminars on warfare, rarely read books on it and even changed the subject when it was brought up. You may laugh, but things got to the stage that I was reluctant to pick up a book on Christian warfare in the shops in case something bad happened.

The Lord was not put off by my shenanigans, and He did not let the matter drop. One day it dawned on me that perhaps I was being attacked because intercession was the very calling the Lord had put on my life! It's funny, isn't it, how it can sometimes take twenty years for the penny to drop? I was so fed up with living with this fear that I cried out, "Well, if I perish, I perish, but come what may, I will trust you, Lord, and do what you are asking me to do!" It was as if a balloon had popped. My faith, weak as it was, had confronted the fear, and it had to go.

There are many ways to deal with fear and stop it from

crippling our lives, calls or destinies. One excellent way is to use the Word of God as ammunition and fire it at any fear entering our minds. Try meditating on these verses, turning them into prayers, songs, fridge magnets or whatever else helps.

> For God did not give us a spirit of timidity (of cowardice, of craven and cringing and fawning fear), but [He has given us a spirit] of power and of love and of calm and well-balanced mind and discipline and self-control.
> —2 TIMOTHY 1:7, AMP

> Perfect love casts out fear.
> —1 JOHN 4:18, NASB

Speaking out the Word of God builds a protective shield of faith that extinguishes the darts of the enemy.

Another way to tackle our fears is to read inspirational stories of people who dared to confront their fears and try the very thing they were afraid of. Louisa May Alcott said, "I am not afraid of storms, for I'm learning how to sail my ship." Virgil Thompson said something similar, "Try a thing you haven't done three times. Once to get over the fear of doing it, twice to learn how to do it, and a third time to figure out whether you like it or not."

If trying these does not bring relief, then get further help to rid you of the fear—and don't let your cringing fears make you afraid of the process!

HEALTHY FEAR

There is a godly fear that is essential for the Christian to have or develop. Cringing fear keeps us from our destinies, but reverential fear sets us free and puts us on its fast track. One ties us up in knots, and the other sets us free. If we make that switch from unhealthy fear to reverential awe, we can take our promised inheritance with both hands.

I will abide in Your tabernacle forever; I will trust in
the *shelter of Your wings.* For You, O God, have heard
my vows; You have given me the *heritage* of those who
fear Your name.
—PSALM 61:4–5, NKJV, EMPHASIS ADDED

Our themes found in Zelophehad's name pop up again in
this verse, bringing together healthy fear or awe, God's shel-
tering wings and our inheritance. Awe is not something that
we can drum up for ourselves; it is a fruit of growing in
understanding the nature of God. It will grow as we get to
know Him more, through spending time with Him, soaking
in His Word and His presence. Sometimes, however, the
Lord comes along and shocks us into deeper awe, taking us
quite by surprise.

Once after a night of praying on a ministry team, I was
asked if I wanted prayer before I headed home. It was late
and I was tired, but we were encouraged not to leave until
we ourselves had been prayed for. I thought that a quick
prayer would not go wrong, and I would soon be tucked up
in my bed. Quite unexpectedly, I sensed the Lord engulfing
me in His presence, and although I could still hear those
about me, I felt alone with Him. I saw a huge dark curtain
and felt a thick presence of the Lord. He asked me, "Do you
want to see My glory?" Before I could respond, an opening
appeared in the middle of the curtain. It was tiny, about the
width of a hair, but what I saw was so powerful, I was left
reeling and unable to articulate what I had seen. I pleaded
with the Lord not to show me any more, and the vision
ended. Of course, I later regretted not having asked to see
more, but at the time the sense of fear and awe was so strong
I could not bear it.

Afterwards, I tried to picture what I had seen and
recreate that feeling, but it was not something I could
muster up for myself. I soon realized that, much as I valued
the experience, spending regular time with the Lord and
plodding away at renewing my mind with His Word was

doing a lot more to grow awe in my life than that one powerful, yet isolated, event. The more awe we have in our lives, the more secure we will be from both enemy attacks and unhealthy fear.

> He who fears the LORD has a secure fortress, and for his children it will be a refuge.
> —PROVERBS 14:26, NIV

For Zelophehad and his contemporaries, the desert was a place of training in trust. Mr. Shadow had to decide if he was to be a shady guy with shady dealings, living in fear for his life, or if he was to be a man living in God's shadow with an attitude of awe.

Zelophehad, "Shadow Fear," feared the Lord enough to not join the rebel ranks. He stood his ground and said no to rebellion and yes to staying in God's protective shadow, conforming to His order.

Not everyone chose as wisely. One of Zelophehad's contemporaries stepped outside the fear of the Lord into shady business. In order to understand the daughters of Zelophehad, we must first meet this rebel, Korah.

CHAPTER 3

Korah

*Our father died in the desert. He was not among
Korah's followers, who banded together against
the Lord.*

—NUMBERS 27:3, NIV

The word was out. Korah was up to something. Earlier that
day the news had spread to Zelophehad's tent and now his
worst suspicions were confirmed. Korah was a man with a
mission, and a growing number realized his mission was to
take Aaron out. For a while now, Zelophehad had seen something in the Levite's eyes that spelled danger. Not everyone had
seen it. From what Zelophehad had heard, many in the tribe
of Reuben were ready to stand alongside Korah and his
cronies. Zelophehad knew Aaron was not a perfect man, but
he also knew the Lord had given him the job and that was
good enough for Zelophehad—all he wanted to do was get on
with his own business, care for his family and get them
through this desert.

"Zelophehad, are you in there?" whispered a voice from
outside. Zelophehad knew who it was and ignored it the first
three times, but the voice was insistent. He crept outside to

lead the man away from his tent so his family would not waken. It was Dathan, one of Korah's henchmen, and he was not easily moved on. Dathan was a leader in his tribe, and he was here at Zelophehad's tent to recruit for Korah's cause.

"I'm not interested, Dathan," Zelophehad said quietly, but with strength in his voice, "Go away; you bring a bad smell to my tent."

Dathan laughed and, ignoring Zelophehad, continued. His tone was smooth, and his talk was slick. It would have sounded convincing to many, but Zelophehad was not taken in.

"Aaron is the Lord's choice, Dathan." Zelophehad heard a child coughing, grabbed Dathan's arm and pulled him farther away from the tent.

"This will only lead to trouble. Remember when Miriam and Aaron confronted Moses?" Even in the shadows of the night, Zelophehad could see a smirk spread across Dathan's face at the mention of Aaron being in trouble with the Lord. "You don't want to be a leper, Dathan," he added. "God's choice is God's choice, and you are on dangerous ground. Now let it be."

"But we are all God's chosen people!" Dathan retorted.

"Dathan," Zelophehad sighed in exasperation, "you are already a prince. What more do you want? To be high priest?" Dathan averted his eyes briefly as Zelophehad continued. "If we have it your way, everyone will want to be high priests."

Dathan persisted a while longer, but soon realized that Zelophehad was not going to budge. He turned away abruptly to go in search of more willing ears. Zelophehad went back to bed but slept little that night. A storm was brewing, and it made him shiver inside.

A MAN IN A MILLION

Every story seems to have a good guy and a bad guy. This one is no different. Zelophehad was a man in a million, assuming half of the Israelites were women. Korah was a man in a million too, but the two men chose to follow very different paths. Both men had come out of Egypt. Both had families. Both are remembered for very different responses to rebellion. One was a popular leader with a charismatic personality who was about to lead many astray. The other was a little-known man who produced women of such character that their impact lasted thousands of years.

Korah was well born, as rebels often are. He was not only a Levite; he was cousin to the Big Guns—Moses and Aaron. His father was Izhar, meaning "shining oil." Translated into modern charismatic vernacular, it would be "resplendent anointing." What a name! Imagine if Korah and Zelophehad had met in kindergarten how they would have compared their dads:

"My dad is anointed, but yours is the pits!"

"Well my dad says being a son of Joseph is better than being a Levite any day!"

Having an anointed Levitical father might have been helpful, but it was not enough to get Korah or anyone else into his promised land. The lineage that counted was the lineage of faith, trust and obedience to the Lord, and each generation had to choose that for themselves.

POSITIONING THE PEOPLE

One of the first jobs the Lord did early in the desert days was to position His people within the camp. (See Numbers 2.) It was not just a matter of picking a tent site anywhere they liked, but obediently going where the Lord placed them. Korah's tribe, the Kohathites, did very well; they got "prime city" living right at the center of things along with the other Levites. Moses and Aaron were just around the corner. Being in the center of camp was a secure position. Any invaders would have to breach thousands of tents before getting to the Kohath suburb.

Imagine if you were in the last tent way out yonder. I

suspect vulnerability levels were higher on the fringes, especially as they bedded down each night. Have you ever felt as if you were on the edge of things? It is part of sinful human nature to jostle and tussle to where the action is. Watch any kids at a sleepover party—they love to cluster in the middle, few want to be the one on the edge.

Circumstances may yell at us that we are being left in the sidelines, and that is how we might feel, but the truth is we are never way out there. Our position is safe and secure in Christ; His tent and ours are supernaturally joined. What better place could there be? We are always in the "in crowd" from the Lord's perspective.

Having said that, geographical position is also important. We must know our station in terms of homes, jobs, churches, cities and nations. If we are unsure of where God wants us to be, then we will indeed feel vulnerable and insecure when trouble hits. There are two words we have to be able to hear clearly from the Lord in terms of positioning. They are short, easy words: *stay* and *go*. We must make sure we know which one the Lord is speaking to us and be obedient to it, even if it is the tougher alternative.

TOP JOBS FOR THE BOYS
(NUMBERS 4:1–20)

After positioning, the Lord deployed His task force and gave them jobs. Of all the Levites, the Kohathites had the most responsible jobs; they took care of the holy things of the tabernacle. (See Numbers 4:4.) It sounds easy, doesn't it? There were four thousand or so able-bodied men just to move a few items. The other Levites had carts to carry the heavy tabernacle curtains and wood, but the Kohathites had to bear their load on their shoulders—symbolic of responsibility and authority. It was a heavy responsibility, but it had its advantages. Each time the cloud moved, Korah and his gang were the last to leave, and by the time they arrived at the new site, the hard work had been done and the tabernacle was set up ready for the furnishings to be put in place.

TOUCH BUT DON'T LOOK!

Responsibility always comes with rules. God's rule for the Kohathites was that, while they could carry the holy items, they were not allowed to look at them. Can you imagine Korah carefully transporting the hidden goods, year in and year out, never getting even a peek into the package resting on his shoulders, or walking over those rocks knowing that if he dropped the load, it would be at his own peril? Just imagine how tense it would have been: there must have been someone to carry the items, someone to catch the carrier in case he fell, and someone to catch the catcher while all the time someone was watching to make sure no one could sneak a look!

Stepping outside the boundaries was Korah's mistake. His power, position and authority in the Hebrew ranks did not satisfy him. A title on a tent flap does not mean the person living inside is pure, and Korah soon revealed his lack of purity. He did not look at the holy items, but he did set his eyes on Aaron's job, revealing a heart that was not pure before the Lord.

David also learned later that, when it came to the ark, curiosity was not allowed. It was a case of integrity or death. (See Numbers 10:21.) This was another serious case of "touch, but don't look!"

We are all called to carry things. We have to know what it is we have to carry, how to carry it and where to carry it. We may be asked to carry a church and take it to the next level of maturity in the Lord. Or it could be a specific task like worship leading, writing a book or feeding the poor. Those are the obvious ones, but what about carrying our families, our communities, cities and nations before the Lord in intercession? No matter what the Lord asks us to carry, His eyes are always focused on our hearts.

Korah

Baldie

Korah means "bald." Perhaps he was born bald and his parents called him "Little Baldie" out of affection. Baldness in the Egyptian culture was a symbol of royalty, so maybe Korah's parents had high ambitions for their son. He certainly had them for himself! But baldness was also a symbol of idolatry.

A bald head is one that is exposed. Exposure is not always bad; Elisha was bald, at least for a time, and he was a great prophet, even though he didn't care much for the title "Baldie"! (See 2 Kings:23–24.) However, metaphorically speaking, in Korah's case, what was in his head was exposed. Stinking thinking always comes out in the end. Korah had more than a close shave with death; his manipulative thoughts cost him his life and the lives of most of his family.

Korah can also be translated as "ice."[1] And his icy antics left such a shiver down the corridors of time that the New Testament issued a strong warning about Korah type of people. Ice is frozen water; it is cold, hard and fixed into shape. It may be made of water, but it is not living, flowing and life giving. What was it that Korah did that was so terrible? In a nutshell, he rebelled.

Rebellion in the Ranks

Rebellion started with Lucifer, infected Adam and continues to this day. The Israelites remained in the desert until rebellion was, at least in part, exchanged for faith. Let's look at three rebellions that preceded the one Korah led.

Rebellion 1: Family feuds (Numbers 11–12)

The first rebellion involved Miriam and Aaron, Moses' older siblings. Miriam and Aaron began to talk against Moses because of his Cushite wife.

"Has the LORD spoken only through Moses?" they asked, "Hasn't he also spoken through us?" And the LORD heard this.

—NUMBERS 12:1–2, NIV

Miriam's and Aaron's argument, picked up years later by their cousin Korah, was about through whom God had chosen to speak. They didn't go to their brother Moses with their grievance but talked behind his back, pulling him down. What led to their sudden outburst? In order to understand their dissatisfaction, we must look at the events that had just taken place.

General discontent had arisen on the camp fringes where the "mixed multitude" lived. These foreigners, complete with their cultural differences, had joined the Israelites on their flight from Egypt but were not happy campers. The Lord nipped their grumbling in the bud by sending fire to encircle the camp perimeter—scary for those in closely packed tents. The Camp Press was still hot with news of the fire when the rumbles started up again, only this time related to a lack of meat. As we shall see later in another chapter, the Lord dealt with the meat issue in two ways; He indeed sent them flesh to eat, (quail that made them sick), but first He sent them the meat of His Word. The latter came through the appointment of seventy prophetic elders. Introducing the prophetic always causes a stir, so can you imagine seventy prophets all at once? It certainly stirred Aaron and Miriam. They responded by attacking Moses' choice of wife.

Zipporah was a Cushite, of foreign stock, as were those on the edge of the camp whose complaints had led to the fire. Aaron and Miriam had not grasped that the issue on the outer fringes was neither cultural nor racial, but one of the heart. By criticizing Zipporah behind Moses' back, they might as well have said directly to their leader, "You should never have married that girl, Moses! You are less than a true Hebrew with her at your side. Think how more important you would be if you had a Hebrew wife!"

KORAH

One argument led to another, and Aaron and Miriam questioned Moses' sole right to speak for God, which was crazy considering Moses had just appointed seventy others to be God's mouthpieces. The prophetic airwaves had never been so full, but still it was not enough for Aaron and Miriam. Perhaps they were just plain angry or jealous that they had not been chosen for the task. It was bad enough having a grumbling, complaining spirit in the people on the outskirts, but now the canker had spread to the camp center, to Moses' family and to God's leaders. The Lord's response was immediate: Miriam was punished with a bout of leprosy and confinement outside the camp. And what was Aaron's punishment? Perhaps it was the intense pain of seeing his younger sister suffer so greatly.

Miriam's isolation was to last seven days, the punishment for a daughter in disgrace. The picture given to us is of a father spitting on his daughter's face, brought on by sin and disgrace. (See Numbers 12:14.) Here the Heavenly Father shows His displeasure by giving Miriam a father's rebuke. It's not something we usually think of—God spitting—but His spit can be healing too, and in the end Miriam, the famous worship leader, was restored.

The shock of all this jolted Aaron and Miriam back into their places. The Lord's message was clear: rebellion, even in the form of grumbling to your younger brother, has consequences. People get burnt, sick and isolated. Cousin Korah looked on, but unfortunately for so many, the lesson passed him by.

Grumbling and resentment affect us in similar ways. What is our favorite grumble zone? Is it, as it was for the people on the outskirts, about our comfort level or material wants? Or is that touchy spot related to the way the Lord is dealing with us?

Complaining to the Lord, or grumbling to or about one another is all sin, the sort of sin that keeps us in the desert.

> Don't grumble against each other, brothers, or you
> will be judged.
> —JAMES 5:9, NIV

The Lord didn't make our bodies to be compatible with constant bitter thoughts and, as it did for Miriam, grumbling can make us sick. The Lord's design was for a contented people, resting and trusting in Him to provide all they would need. Godliness with contentment always brings great gain. (See 1 Timothy 6:6–8.) Paul grasped this well:

> I have learned the secret of being content in any and
> every situation, whether well fed or hungry, whether
> living in plenty or in want. I can do everything
> through him who gives me strength.
> —PHILIPPIANS 4:12–13, NIV

REBELLION 2: TROUBLE IN THE HIGHLANDS (NUMBERS 14–15)

Caleb, Joshua and ten others returned from their sortie into the Promised Land. The twelve spies had been charged with a big responsibility—they held in their hands the prophetic promises of a nation. When they came back dirty, tired and fearful, the crowds swarmed to the center of the camp to hear their report. Zelophehad and his wife waited with racing hearts for word to be passed back through the throngs. They knew that the future of their family hinged on a good report. Korah, as one of the leadership, was fortunate to hear the report firsthand and see, touch and smell the fruit of the land.

The long-awaited report brought confusion, fear and disappointment. Yes, there was milk and honey, but there were also fortified cities filled with strong and powerful people. Word spilled back quickly to the masses.

"Giants!"

"Devourers!"

"Grasshoppers?"

KORAH

"Enemies!"

Within minutes it looked as if a riot was about to break out. Caleb stood up, and his voice roared like a lion over the noise.

"We can do it, people. Listen to me, we can still do it!"

The crowd gradually quieted, partly because the strength of Caleb's voice astonished them and also because hope, dashed so quickly at the report of a powerful enemy, raised its head once more.

But the new hope did not last long. That night the Canvas City mourned bitterly. The noise of their crying rose and fell like a demonic orchestra, and by morning they were ready to return to Egypt—under an entirely new leadership.

Korah, of course, was more than ready to suggest who that new leader should be, but before he could present his curriculum vitae, things got even crazier. Moses and Aaron were lying on the ground weeping yet again.

"When I am leader, I will never waste time sobbing like a baby in a sandpit," he thought to himself.

Caleb and Joshua added to the drama of the day by wandering around half-naked, clothing torn to shreds. "Disgraceful!" hissed Korah to Dathan, "and if Joshua ben Nun says 'exceedingly good' one more time, I am going to personally stone him!"

Korah and Dathan bent down and picked up stones. Others noticed and followed their example. The tension and noise mounted, and the only ones who did not seem to notice were Moses and Aaron who were still fervently praying in the sand.

Korah was not expecting what happened next. God showed up—and stunned them all into silence. Moses went alone into the Tent of Meeting, and the terrified people waited for yet another report. A strange weight in the air seemed to immobilize Korah, and he could not have opened his mouth if he tried.

Moses came out of the tent bringing his report with him. There was good news and bad news. The good news was that, in the face of impending judgment, Moses had pleaded for their lives and had won a reprieve for all except the ten faithless

43

spies. The bad news? They would have to live the rest of their lives in the desert.[1]

Pain and grief muddied the waters and caused more stinking thinking to come to the surface. The Hebrews brooded their fate overnight. Some in the community woke early, got together and decided to take matters into their own hands.

"OK! Let's take the land, then. Who's coming with me?"

"The Lord wants us to be bold? I will show Him how bold I am!"

"Caleb and Joshua were right after all. Let's go!"

It sounds good, doesn't it? After all, wasn't that what God wanted? Not entirely. In their urgency to avoid punishment, these people ignored the instruction not to move until God moved—and the Cloud had not yet moved. They had also moved without their God-appointed leaders.

The rebels, in their presumption, set out to take the highlands. Going ahead of the Lord, of course, spelled disaster. The enemy easily overcame them, and they came back beaten and bruised from the attack. The Lord wanted to give His people more instruction on how to take the land—His way.

The highland go-getters were not the only presumptuous ones. Presumption was one of Korah's weaknesses, and although he had not raced off for the mountains, the seeds of rebellion were growing in his heart. No matter what Moses, God or anyone else said, Korah was not prepared to spend the rest of his life in the desert.

Fortunately for us, we don't have to spend our lives going around in desert circles. But dry, testing days will come to grow us—Jesus Himself had to spend time in the wilderness, after all—and we must be careful that we do not try to get out of those difficult days by relying on our own strength or acting presumptuously.

There are many ways we try to do this, including planning instead of praying, by rushing instead of waiting or by speaking instead of listening. And pray, wait, listen we must, because it is the voice of the Lord that shakes the desert out of us—and us out of the desert. (See Psalm 29:8.) Presumption and self-reliance want us to grab what we can *now* even if we are not ready for it.

There will be a time when He says, "Time to go," or "Take your promises now." But until then, perhaps the Lord wants to do a little more work with us in the desert first.

REBELLION 3: LITTLE MATCHES, BIG BLAZES

The desert is not all work and no play, however. The Lord gave important instructions for weekly rest—a time especially to consider what holiness involved. Breaking God's laws brought consequences, not just to an individual who sinned, but to those around him. Big fires can be started with little matches, and that is what happened in the next rebellion.

A man had gone wood collecting for the day. It was the Sabbath, however, and gathering wood was breaking the law. Moses sought the Lord about the matter; the penalty for this willful sin was death by stoning. Many people who loved this man must have been in a state of deep grief as his punishment was carried out.

The Lord had an idea to help the people keep their hearts and minds on Him—sky-blue tassels on their clothing to remind them not to look at the earth but at the heavens, so that any time they looked down, they would be encouraged to lift their eyes to God!

Suddenly, tassel makers were in great demand. Imagine the cooperation needed to quickly make two million tassels! Blue swinging accessories were in fashion, but Korah and some of his friends in leadership quickly forgot that the outer garment was just a reminder of the inner changes needed. And this little match between Moses and the wood-cutter was just what Korah needed to kindle a larger fire.

To us, it may seem pretty harsh to stone a man for picking

up some sticks. Fortunately, we live on this side of the cross and won't get stoned for gathering wood, but the Lord may well "haul us up" for lighting other kinds of fires. And most of the "fires" in the camp were caused by one thing:

> We all make many mistakes, but those who control their tongues can also control themselves in every other way. We can make a large horse turn around and go wherever we want by means of a small bit in its mouth. And a tiny rudder makes a huge ship turn wherever the pilot wants it to go, even though the winds are strong. So also, the tongue is a small thing, but what enormous damage it can do. A tiny spark can set a great forest on fire. And the tongue is a flame of fire. It is full of wickedness that can ruin your whole life. It can turn the entire course of your life into a blazing flame of destruction, for it is set on fire by hell itself.
>
> —JAMES 3:2–6, NLT

KORAH'S REBELLION

All around the camp, tongues flickered like flames in a fire. Korah was delighted when news reached his tent that many well-respected community leaders were prepared to come alongside him. He threw a "party" and gathered them together. "Moses has gone just too far this time," he declared after some pleasantries had been exchanged, "someone has to lead us in stopping him before he destroys us all." He scoured the tent for a raised hand but, as he had hoped, found none. "Well, then, I guess it comes down to me!"

The people were feeling very disgruntled about the Lord's recent decision to let them die in the desert. The woodcutter incident, on top of everything else, had created such a stir that two hundred fifty-three community leaders were now ready, in their insolence, to confront Moses and Aaron. The pot had been heating up over a long time, each incident raising the temperature a few more degrees and each adding a few more converts to Korah's way of thinking. Now that the pot was at the boil, Korah was in his element. Now he had plenty of men of power on his side. Korah "rose up" and went to Moses, his spiritual intimidation team tagging along with him.

> Korah son of Izhar, the son of Kohath, the son of Levi, and certain Reubenites—Dathan and Abiram, sons of Eliab, and On son of Peleth—became insolent and rose up against Moses. With them were 250 Israelite men, well-known community leaders who had been appointed members of the council. They came as a group to oppose Moses and Aaron and said to them, "You have gone too far! The whole community is holy, every one of them, and the *Lord* is with them. Why do you set yourselves above the *Lord's* assembly?"
> —NUMBERS 16:1–3, NIV

Moses knew that this "special council meeting" was going to be no picnic. Each of the men before him represented several thousand people.

Rising up is not always bad. We are told to rise up many times in Scripture. The good uprising leads to taking new ground in our lives, and it is for the kingdom of God. We have to rise up in God's way and in God's time and with His nature written on our hearts. Korah, in his rebellious leadership challenge, missed the mark on all three points.

KORAH'S COMPLAINTS

The best thing Korah, as a leader, could have done for his clan was to model godly behavior in the face of God's decisions. But he chose the opposite path. Now he stood outside Moses' tent, blind to the fact that his fight was not against Moses but against the Lord. Insolence, the heart of rebellion, is rooted in pride and arrogance and often speaks in spiritual language.

Sometimes it has an intellectual flavor in which head knowledge and smooth articulation blend to intimidate, and Korah was an expert at this. With his grievance committee standing close behind him, he was ready to speak.

DESERT PETITION

COMPLAINT 1: Moses has gone too far.
COMPLAINT 2: All God's people are holy and chosen.
COMPLAINT 3: Moses is no better than anyone else.

Signed,
Korah the Kohathite
and 250 others

Let's look more closely at the complaints.

Complaint 1: Moses has gone too far.

Moses, who had heard correctly on the woodcutter issue, was more concerned about pleasing God than two million grumblers. Korah, however, was a people-pleaser, with the person he most wanted to please being himself. His point was not really that Moses had gone too far, but that Moses had not gone far enough—in making Korah his top man.

(Let's be honest, most of us at some point have said, "They've gone a bit too far!" I know I have, though probably most of the time what I am actually saying is, "I don't like the way this is being done.")

Complaint 2: All God's people are holy and chosen.

Korah's argument was that before the Lord everyone was equal, chosen and holy. Korah had a grasp of New Testament truth here, but for all his holy talk, he was not displaying evidence of it in his own life. Maybe he was tired of carrying things he may not look at on his shoulders. Korah wanted to see. He wanted to touch. He wanted cousin Aaron's job in the Holy Place, and if everyone were equally holy, that would justify his ambition! Korah was twisting truth to suit his own needs.

(This manipulative behavior, disguised in theological-sounding apparel, leaves a trail of destruction in its wake. Sooner or later this sort of inner discontent and selfish thinking is exposed and is seen for what it is, but it may cause a lot of damage in the meantime.)

Complaint 3: Moses is no better than anyone else.

Korah was accusing Moses of getting it wrong by lording it over others. This must have stung Moses because it hit an old wound from many years before. Remember when Moses, fresh from murdering an Egyptian, saw his fellow Hebrews fighting and tried to sort out the trouble? The Hebrews had retorted, "Who made you ruler and judge over us?" (Exod. 2:14, NIV). Aaron and Miriam touched the scar, and now here was Korah striking the same spot. The Lord had forgiven Moses for his sin, but the enemy would use it for as long as he could. This challenge must have made Moses wince and say "Oh, no, not THAT again!"

Korah was challenging Moses' right to lead and his delegation of authority to Aaron. Behind his statement was a hidden agenda taunting, "Look at me. Can't you see I would do a better job than Aaron or Moses?" It is true that Moses was a sinner, a man like everyone else, but it was faulty reasoning for Korah to assume he should be co-leader.

(That's just like Satan, isn't it, to bring up past issues? We all have battle wounds and scars, sometimes caused by our own sin. Satan accuses us and makes us think we are unfit for service. And the Korahs also bring up the old stuff, throwing it in our faces. But our past does not disqualify us from our destiny. We are all sinners, saved by grace, our leaders included. And their task in handling the Korahs is not a pleasant one.)

Korah had confronted Moses, the man who once hated public speaking, with great eloquence. The speech impressed many, but not Moses, not Zelophehad and certainly not God. Zelophehad would have nothing to do with complaining or the complainant. He saw through Korah and stood quietly in the shadows, teaching and training his girls in manners as well as godliness—with Korah as an excellent example of how not to behave. Zelophehad was content to follow God's chosen leadership and remain faithful to his simple position as a responsible law-abiding father of five girls in the suburb of Manasseh.

MOSES' REACTION TO REBELLION

Moses had already dealt with the Miriam-Aaron rebellion, but at least that involved only two people. Korah's rebellion again hit very close to home but involved many more: his cousin, fellow worshipers and friends. These were the people he had walked with on his journeys and talked with until late at night under the warmth of the fire.

How would you respond, leader or not, to such a confrontation? Shout, yell or argue, reason or restrict, debate or control? Moses' reaction was to fall down and pray before the Lord. When Moses fell on his face and wept, his tears were not to manipulate people to his side emotionally. They were tears of humility and intercession. There on the desert sands he sought God and heard Him speak once again. By the time he stood up, he had been given wisdom for the situation. Korah was the one who had gone too far, not Moses.

Moses instructed Korah and all his company to come before the Lord the following morning with their censers swinging, and the Lord would point out who was holy. Everyone was in for a long, hard night, and the gossipers were in full force guessing who said what and what would happen next.

KORAH

Next morning, all of Korah's cohorts except Dathan and Abiram turned up in front of the Tent of Meeting. The whole assembly was in absolute silence as Moses, on the Lord's instruction, told the others to separate themselves from Korah and his men and stand away from the tents of Korah, Dathan and Abiram. As the congregation watched, earthquakes took out the tents, swallowing up the men, their wives, children and all their possessions. A wave of fire then consumed the two hundred and fifty others who had taken part.

Korah, the icy bald one, was gone, but the complaining spirit was not. You would think the people would have learned from the previous day's earthquake, but the very next day the dissension started again. (See Numbers 16:41.) Their grief shouted louder than their ability to hear what the Lord was saying through the earthquake, and they rebelled once more.

In all, nearly fifteen thousand people perished.

So many lost their lives that day that a revised census was necessary. The time frame between the deaths and the new census is not known, but we do know Zelophehad died before it took place. Without sons, his name could not be counted, or so it seemed. But because he had been content to stay in the fear of the Lord, his immediate offspring were richly blessed (even though they were women). Some of Korah's offspring, by the mercy of God, survived and were still blessed, although it was some years before they were granted positions of authority again as worship leaders under David.

Korah and Zelophehad: men of the desert. I think this verse sums up these two men perfectly:

> Blessed is the man who always fears the LORD, but he who hardens his heart falls into trouble.
> —PROVERBS 28:14, NIV

Moses, also a "man of the desert," displayed more fear of the Lord than anyone else in his generation. He had become the most humble man in the whole earth, wholly reliant on God. And he was blessed. The Lord never let him down when he asked for wisdom and help in leading the motley crew through the desert.

Sometimes wisdom, in a time of crisis, is found only as we fall on our faces, noses in the dirt and sand in our eyes. Speaking as a contact lens wearer, I can tell you that sand in my eyes makes me cry! What is the first port of call for good leaders when rebellion hits the ranks? It's not to fight to maintain control or rush committee meetings that will react in the flesh. It's not to dig out the best sermons on submission and authority. It is to humbly call upon the Lord and then listen to what He says.

THE KORAH SPIRIT

Speaking out, even about leadership decisions—just as in rising up—is not always wrong; Zelophehad's daughters challenged their leaders concerning the law, but the Lord said they "spoke rightly." Rebellious Korah is an example of wrong speaking out. He was such a serious troublemaker that he gets a mention in the New Testament.

Jude reminds us of three rebellions: the angelic uprising in heaven, Sodom and Gomorrah and Korah's rebellion, and he links Korah to Cain and Balaam. The common thread is rejection of authority, but these men share other attributes, mentioned in Jude's short letter. They must:

1. Be able to slip in secretly without drawing attention to themselves—at first! (See Jude 4.)

2. Express the doctrine of grace eloquently but use it as a license for immoral living. (See Jude 4.)

3. Pretend to know Christ, but deny His Lordship. (See Jude 4.)

4. Be seasoned at rejecting authority. (See Jude 6.)

5. Be experienced in slandering celestial beings. (See Jude 8.)

6. Be able to hurl abuse at anything they don't understand. (See Jude 10.)

7. Pretend to be a good shepherd (but at love feasts feed only themselves). (See Jude 12.)

8. Be good at promising but not delivering (especially schemes and dreams). (See Jude 12.)

9. Be ungodly in action and speech. (See Jude 15.)

10. Show strong aptitude for grumbling, fault finding, flattery, boasting and scoffing. (See Jude 16.)

11. Be able to cause division. (See Jude 19.)

Jude gives us three word pictures to illustrate his point about these ungodly dissenters. Firstly, a person like Korah—or Cain or Balaam—is like a cloud without rain. (See Jude 12.) He looks promising but does not deliver the goods. He brings hope of refreshment only to dash it again. His words may sound spiritual enough, but they do not release any life-giving water.

Again, the Korah spirit, Jude says, is like an autumn tree "without fruit and uprooted—twice dead" (Jude 12, NIV). An uprooted tree is a sad sight. What was once alive, upright and strong, now lies in the dirt, dead at both ends. Yes, the tree is still there, but it is exposed at the roots. All that is left is wood and bark. The Korah tree, once with such potential for growth, is uprooted and revealed for what it is—a hollow, empty core.

In the last image, Jude says men (or women) like this are like "wild waves of the sea, foaming up their shame" (Jude 13, NIV). I've often walked along Scottish beaches laced with foam. This sort of foam is colorless empty froth. It's neither sea nor sand, and it's messy. Stand on it, and it collapses because there is no substance to it at all.

Those with a spirit of Korah are likened by Jude to huge pus-filled boils that seep poison into loving fellowship in the family of God. (See Jude 12.) People with a Korah spirit have no qualms about eating with a person one day and cutting him down the next. The Korah "shepherds" choose to feed themselves while their flocks go hungry. They muddle leadership and appointment and seek power for its own sake.

Jude ends his letter by giving four strategies for those facing up to a Korah type of person:

1. Build yourself up in your faith. (See Jude 20.)

2. Pray in the Holy Spirit. (See Jude 20.)

3. Keep waiting in God's love. (See Jude 21.)

4. Be merciful, remembering Christ's mercy to you, but mix it with fear. (See Jude 21–22.)

Your Korah might disappear into some giant crack in the ground of his own making—or he might end up repenting.

An opportunity

Those who died in the aftermath of Korah's death, the fifteen thousand who rebelled, all missed an opportunity. Yes, things had been tough with the earthquake and the fires. But every painful circumstance offered them a chance to listen to the Lord and obey. The very dust of the earth was crying out for them to repent, but their hearts were hardened and they paid with their lives.

> Today, if you will hear His voice, do not harden your hearts as in the rebellion; in the day of trial in the wilderness.
>
> —HEBREWS 3:7, NKJV

Today. It cannot be put off until tomorrow. If we do not listen to God right here and now, then it will be harder for us to hear Him next time because our hearts will be that little bit harder. And if our hearts are soft, and we can discern His voice easily, we will be able to hear when He says, "Now! Time to make your next move into your destiny!"

With the census upon them, the daughters of Zelophehad seized the opportunity and made their move. Let's meet the first of them now.

CHAPTER 4

Mahlah

Zelophehad came out of his tent to face the small crowd and, shaking his head, said only two words, "Still nothing." He drew a deep breath and then disappeared back into the tent.

It had been an anxious labor, and his young wife's cries of pain woke people as far as ten tents away. Older women muttered their advice through the canvas fabric until they had run out of counsel. Wise old men spent the evening discussing names to suggest to Zelophehad, but with each passing hour their names seemed more and more irrelevant. Younger mothers tried to get their offspring back to bed, but amongst them a party atmosphere had developed, and children were running around everywhere, playing and dancing in the moonlight.

The last hour, however, had been a silent one. Parents carried tired children back to bed and returned with blankets for those who pleaded to stay up. They sat sleepily, huddled together, *oblivious to the concern around them, waiting for that first cry.*

But it was Zelophehad's appearance with a tiny bundle in his arms that brought everyone to their feet. Choking with conflicting emotions, he announced softly, "It's a girl."

Holding the baby tenderly, he folded back the swaddling to give those pressing around him a first peek. The moonlight shone softly on her face to show a quiet, frail little baby with little life in her.

"Her name is Mahlah," Zelophehad said slowly, his voice cracking with pain. The children took a look at the delicate infant and drifted back to their beds, none the wiser.

A few sensitive women stroked the baby's cheek and briefly cooed and crooned knowingly. Zelophehad nodded in appreciation then moved back into the tent, his joy dulled by stabbing fears that his daughter would not make it through her first night. And the wise old men nodded thoughtfully and agreed Mahlah was a very apt name indeed.

MAHLAH: DISEASE AND HEALING

Mahlah means "sickness or disease." In a culture where names were highly significant, it is likely that Zelophehad's baby girl was born with some sort of malady. If so, her parents would have questioned what God was up to—after all, hadn't the Lord promised His people a disease-free journey?

> If you listen carefully to the voice of the LORD your God and do what is right in his eyes…I will not bring on you any of the diseases I brought on the Egyptians, for I am the LORD who heals you.
> —EXODUS 15:26, NIV

A disease-free society was God's primary health plan for His people. But it was conditional upon being in obedient relationship to Him. So, is sickness then caused by disobedience? Is healing only for those who know Him? Why does an innocent baby arrive into the world tainted with pain? These questions are rooted in real life situations for so many and often are the very struggles that keep many in their deserts.

Though we might not like to hear it, sin and sickness are connected. Adam and Eve knew that. Before the fall there was no death, no sick relationships, no pain. And as long as there is sin in the world, there will still be sickness. But the Lord has a remedy; He is *Jehovah Rapha*, "the Lord who heals."

Being the Healer is an intrinsic part of His nature—that's why Jesus went around curing so many people, quietly saying, through many miracles, "I can heal. I do heal. I will heal."

So what does He heal? Firstly, He restores our broken relationship with the Father through the power of the cross. That spiritual healing ensures us everlasting life, complete with new, perfect never-to-be-sick-again bodies.

God also heals our emotions of the traumas and horrors "Egypt" inflicts on us, establishing peace and freedom in our hearts. Whatever damage we have suffered in our past, we can be restored.

And then there is the healing of our bodies. No matter what our personal theology is on physical healing, a lot of it happens in the Bible. So why do we, especially in the Western world, not see more of it today? I asked a few friends what they thought about this. Here are some of the answers I received:

"We don't see many healings because we don't pray enough for the sick."

"People don't have enough faith or don't stand on the promises of God."

"Some people need to sort out their inner lives before God will touch their bodies by releasing forgiveness and bitterness."

"We need more of the anointing in the church and more people with the gift of healing who exercise it."

"We have too lowly a view of who God is and of His power to heal."

"Churches don't make enough room for the Holy Spirit to move."

"Sometimes it looks as if God is *not* healing, when part of His plan is to develop character in us."

"Christians don't understand that Jesus died for our diseases as well as our sins."

So what answer would you give?

Whatever our view, the Bible encourages us to pray for the sick, with assurances of answered prayer. And that is what I try to do. I don't confess to having all the answers, but I do know that we need to be praying more for the sick, rather than just sitting back discussing the theology of it. And since one of God's names is Healer, then praying with believing hearts that He can and wants to heal is a good place to start, and then let Him work out how He will answer our prayer.

When a friend calls for a chat and happens to mention she has a sore throat, we should stop and pray for her. When a colleague has been off work for a few days, we might send an e-mail to him to let him know we are thinking about him and are praying for his welfare.

Become a hospital chaplain or voluntary worker; offer prayer to strangers in the street who look as if they need it; make sure our neighbors know we will pray when they need it. Instead of waiting for the sick to come to the church to find the healing power of Jesus, let's take the church to the people and get the gift of healing out into the highways and byways of life!

Encourage and pray for your Christian doctors and nurses, who lay hands on people every day. Wouldn't it be fantastic for every patient to be prayed for before surgery and see a good few of them released without needing anything done because God had intervened? Does your heart, like mine, groan with longing to see an explosion of healing power in and through the church? Maybe the answer lies in our own hands as we lay them upon the sick and ask the Lord to heal.

People who regularly visit developing nations testify to

seeing many more dramatic miracles in those needy lands. Perhaps, in deserts of poverty and injustice, hearts are better prepared for a manifestation of God's power. Before you pack your bags and move to India (although that might be a very good place to learn more about healing), let me share two stories of ways God has worked healing into the lives of friends of mine.

SUE'S FOOT

Sue, an Australian friend, had been burnt badly as a child and suffered severe scarring on her foot. It was permanently arched into a tight ball, the bottom of the foot pulled up, the toes underneath it like claws. This made walking very tiring. Having a badly scarred foot for so many years was a desert experience for Sue. Then the Lord started to stir her about a missionary trip to Russia, but it involved a lot of walking, and Sue didn't know how she would be able to handle it. One evening she arrived at home group to find everyone was removing their shoes because of heavy rain. People, of course, noticed her scarred foot for the first time and asked how it happened. A tearful Sue explained, and during a coffee break, the Lord told a woman to kiss and embrace Sue's foot.

She went home, her heart flooded with mixed emotions, and told her husband about the meeting then headed to bed. She woke during the night to visit the bathroom and glanced down at her foot. The discoloration had gone and the foot lay flat, toes straight on the floor. Her cries of excitement and joy woke her family. When I met her the next morning, she was radiant! Sue had to wait a while for her miracle, and when it came, it was quietly over coffee and just in time for Russia, a trip that opened the way for a whole new ministry for her family.

So why did the Lord wait to heal her? Was it to do with faith or obedience? I doubt it. I know this lady, and faith and obedience were not lacking in her life. For Sue it was a matter of patience, trust and the Lord's timing as she watered her mustard seed and prayed about her mountain and the call to Russia. The waiting period can often be the fast track to our destinies as the pains and strains of our personal weaknesses or sicknesses drive us closer to the Lord. When healing eventually came for Sue, it caught her completely by surprise.

CODY AND ELIJAH

Mark and Wendy live in the U.S.A. and have two boys who were born with spina bifida. The nerve damage means that they have little or no feeling in their lower body. Cody, age nine, and Elijah, age four, have had between them twenty corrective surgeries, twice both boys having surgery at the same time. Wendy, who also miscarried five babies, wrote this to me:

> My boys have blessed me so much. They have shown me such love, and I see incredible strength and peace within them. For all they have been through, they have never complained or asked why. That has really made me look at my own reactions to things. I have not been through nearly what they have, and yet I moan and complain.
>
> Having two children with special needs has brought me to my knees, and that is so fulfilling. My heart is now bent toward those who are sick, especially as I pray for them.
>
> Cody recently reached out to encourage a kid from church who went through some major operations. Seeing him share his own experiences with someone else was such a blessing to me. And my little Elijah...he has such a sensitive spirit. He is so gentle and compassionate. With braces and crutches, he is my singing and dancing buddy as we worship together each day before the Lord. I don't know what God's plan is for my boys, but I thank Him for holding them firmly in His grip.

In spite of so much suffering, Mark, Wendy, Cody and Elijah are able to thank God for the answers to prayer they have seen so far. And they continue to pray, gratefully receiving their boys' healing in small steps and little packages.

Healing is there for us all, and it comes in many different packages. Some are healed bit by bit, while others, like Sue, receive it more dramatically. Others, for whatever reasons, do not get the physical healing package they asked for until glory, but find instead an inheritance of inner peace, strength, courage, empathy and much more.

We do not know whether Mahlah received a healing or plodded through the desert with some infirmity all her life, but whatever happened, we know she didn't let anything hold her back from her destiny—to be an inheritor.

Mahlah and Weakness

Mahlah would be better written *Machalah* (the *ch* pronounced with a gutteral sound as in the Scottish *loch*). It can be broken up to give two root words: *machal* and *chalah*. Firstly, *chalah* means "to be weak, grieved, wounded, sore and tired." Poor girl! What a way to start life.

Imagine little Mahlah in the desert kindergarten with her friends sporting beautiful names like Rachel ("little ewe") and Hannah ("gift of God"). Can you hear them calling out after her in the desert sandpits?

"Weakling, come here!"

"We don't want Disease on our team!"

"Freaky Weaky! You're just a freak!"

Mahlah was not so different from so many of us who start off disadvantaged. She was born in a desert. As a child she had known tiredness, weakness and sore legs. Her teenage years had been wrecked by the rebellions, which led to far more years in the sandpit than any kid should know. She lived in a culture that was unsure of where they were headed and how long the journey would take.

Mahlah

Any lengthy journey taken with children brings familiar cries to parents' ears of "Are we there yet? How much longer, Daddy?" Mahlah was a daughter of Zelophehad. Her daddy said that she was going to go places and live in a land of milk and honey. Mahlah believed what her daddy said; otherwise, she would not have risked her life trying to get there. Mahlah may have started out weak, but eventually she became a world changer.

What Daddy Said

Some people seem to have it going against them from the start. Born into tough lives through no fault of their own, they can spend much of their lives trying to break the various cycles of rejection, pain or suffering.

We all have desert experiences sooner or later. The route from bondage to destiny passes through the wildernesses of testing circumstances, whether physical, emotional or spiritual. Weariness may creep in along with dryness, doubt and discouragement. We yearn to leave the sandpits and war against giants of the land instead, but our feet seem barely capable of taking the next step. These are tough days. And then on top of everything else, the desert winds expose the sinfulness of our hearts, and we wonder if we will live through the painful refining process. Our hearts tell us we are destined for something more, but our minds battle a taunting voice that suggests we will never get there.

What is it that the enemy shouts, or even whispers, in our ears to ridicule our weakness and keep us as cripples? Is it the "You'll never make it!" line? Or does he try, "You'll always be weak or sick; nothing is going to change"?

Satan is a liar. To silence him, we must know what our Father has said about the various journeys we are on. The Bible is the road map we need to get from our deserts to our destiny, and the Lord is our Guide. For particular seasons in our lives, the Lord will emphasize a part of that map by giving us a prophetic word. These words can come to us quietly while we are alone or through someone else, over a cup of coffee or during a meeting at church. There are many ways the Lord chooses to speak. These prophetic words will never contradict the Word of God, but will act like a high-lighter pen over the top of it, building an extra measure of hope, encouragement and exhortation.

When we are in a desert season, exhausted and tired, we can allow those promises to collect dust and forget what the Father has said, but this is the time we need to stand on them more than ever!

WHAT HAS HE PROMISED US?

Our Bibles and our prophetic words have to be dug out, read through and prayed into. This is not as much hard work as it sounds. Even if you have never had a prophetic word in your life, just find something you are promised in the Bible but do not yet see. Talk to the Lord about it, ask Him why you are not seeing it so far, and as long as all your ducks are in a row, trust He will answer. Stand in front of the mirror and tell yourself that promise is coming until faith breaks loose in your heart.

I enjoy doing this in creative ways. We have a large painting of poppies in our hallway at home as a reminder of God's desire for each of us to grow to our full potential. The smallest, straggliest poppy represents me, just in case I should be accused of wanting to be a tall poppy. (People who live in Australia understand the "tall poppy syndrome": anyone who rises above others in some way needs to be brought back down to size.) I often point to the "Wendy" poppy in the picture and say, "Grow in Jesus name!" My kids shake their heads and laugh at me, but when I feel weak or discouraged, it stirs faith in my heart. My strange antics may never rub off on my family, but hopefully the tall poppy painting will always remind them that God wants them to grow to their fullest potential. And if any of the other poppies in the field, apart from my family, want to grow tall too—that's fine by me.

Weakened for a Season, Weakened for a Reason

The process of spiritual growth is not easy and involves growing pains. It can be hard to sense what God is doing in us in this season. Yes, sometimes it is our own foolishness that brings us low, but at other times the Lord allows things to happen to us because He knows it will grow us stronger. God is a loving Father; He does not do this harshly, to punish us and drive us into the ground. He does it to soften our hearts and enable the seed of destiny to grow and bear fruit in our lives. That's what He was doing taking the Israelites through the desert. He wanted to evict their fears and doubts and fill the space as He did for Joshua and Caleb, with boldness and courage! The desert, if we will let it, will put steel into our spiritual backbones.

> In the wilderness He fed you manna which your fathers did not know, that He might humble you and that He might test you, to do good for you in the end.
> —Deuteronomy 8:16, NASB

Weakness and the Journey to the Throne

Paul was a man who knew weakness and learned how to embrace it with open arms! He did not respond to his troubles with a pity party but instead with a firm grasp of God's spiritual dynamics of how to turn weakness into strength.

This is one of God's specialties. Through the cross He allowed Himself to be weak in order to show us His power. The cross becomes our route to strength. To live properly we must die to self. To gain all we want, we must give it away. God would rather use our weaknesses than our strengths to build His kingdom. Why? "So that no one may boast before him" (1 Cor. 1:29).

Arrogance says, "I can do it! I'm gifted! Look at me!" When we do it God's way, we say, "Help, I'm weak, and I can't do it! I will step out trusting Him, shaking in my boots, then He will show up, and there will be no question about who is doing the work!"

You may say, "Well, I'm not weak, I am just plain tired and fed up with all the pressures around me. It's depressing. Work pressure. Spiritual warfare. Family life. Messy church life!" Paul knew about all those too.

> We were under great pressure, far beyond our ability
> to endure, so that we despaired even of life. Indeed in
> our hearts we felt the sentence of death.
> —2 CORINTHIANS 1:8

Hardly anyone could beat Paul's list of troubles: hard work, rejection, accusation, misunderstanding, floggings, stonings, beatings and shipwrecks, flooded, pursued, little sleep, hard work, not a lot of food and sometimes no clothes. This was "Survivor in the Outback" at its most testing! As if that wasn't bad enough, his church was facing growing pains! Paul builds towards this final trouble, as if the last one beats the lot. (See 2 Corinthians 11.)

And then he says, I imagine with a sparkle in his eye, "I know a man…who was caught up to the third heaven" (2 Cor. 12:2).

Happily for Paul, his list is followed by a profound throne room experience. We pray to have an experience like this, but we tend to forget that these follow on the heels of our weaknesses, not our strengths.

The most powerful times I have had with the Lord have been when I was at my lowest. I will never forget the night the Lord came and carried me up on His wings.

I had been through a devastating series of events in my life. One after the other they toppled down on me until I felt so crushed I thought I would never recover. I decided to visit a few close friends in the U.S.A. and take some time out to catch my breath. The trip was planned, but before I could leave, more was to topple around me. One of the friends I was going to see died suddenly. In the week before my trip, I discovered a breast lump and went to see a doctor who told me she had other concerns and sent me off for tests, so two days before departure I was having a body scan. Our eldest daughter, Shaeron, had flown the nest to take a year in missions and, after two weeks away, was very homesick. My husband was on a missions trip to India and called to say he had been in an earthquake. "I'm OK. We're not at the epicenter, but pray because they're expecting more shocks to come!"

By now it was time to go, and I had little emotional and physical strength left. Packing a suitcase, even for this seasoned traveler, was the last straw, and my daughter Kirstine came to my rescue. As I lay on my bed watching her organize my case, I wondered if I was crazy to even try to go. But inside me there was a gentle fluttering of the Spirit of God, saying, "You can do it; I want you on this trip."

After a few days at the International House of Prayer in Kansas City, my second stop took me to the World Prayer Center in Colorado Springs. This was where Lois and I had planned to catch up, enjoy a good conference and chatter into the night. Now she was unexpectedly with the Lord; I was far from home and, even with the hotel buzzing with intercessors, felt very alone. As I lay on my bed, a worship song about soaring with God playing into my ears, I wept, crying out to the Lord, "Oh, God, I feel as if I will never fly again! My heart is hurting so much!"

In my mind I could see my wings wrapped tightly around my heart to protect it from further pain. As I wept I heard the songs playing and, although I could still hear the female singer's voice, superimposed on it was the Lord's. Time seemed to stand still as He sang to me, each line in response to a cry. His voice was gentle, soothing and loving. He sang of my flying again, soaring again, rising again, and slowly I felt Him take my "wings" from around my heart and flood it with warm oil. Then, I felt scooped up onto the back of the Holy Spirit, my wings outstretched over His, and we took off. As He soared I was transported into the heights of heaven. And all the time Jesus was singing, "You will soar again! You will fly!" We flew together for a long, long time, twirling over mountains, rivers, seas, up and down until eventually He placed me gently back on my bed.

Outwardly nothing had changed. My friend was still gone; I was still returning to see specialists and to face the pain of the situations I had left. But inside something had changed; I had been given a new perspective. I had soared with Jesus, in His strength and not my own—and I had tasted of His sweet love. And I tell you, my season of weakness was worth it for the flight!

Mahlah and Grief

So Mahlah, through her name, reminds us of sickness and healing, weakness and strength, but the name also means grief, and Zelophehad's firstborn tasted its bitter depths.

A season of grief is one of the hardest to cope with. It visits us in many ways, often without warning and sometimes it arrives—just like it did above—when we are already very weary. Grief is a byproduct of loss: loss of a loved one, a job or a friendship but also loss of freedom or hope. Grief is a deep wound that takes the color out of our lives turning everything dismal. We wonder when we are in that gray season if we will ever truly recover. The birds have not stopped singing, but we rarely hear their songs. The trees still blossom, but their branches seem bare. Overwhelming loss and pain cloud each day, and broken hearts are stabbed with questions until they become numb.

No matter what calamity or loss has thrown us into a

river of grief, there is an inheritance found in swimming its course. Just as weakness is replaced by God's strength, and sickness with healing power, grief is eventually replaced with joy.

> Weeping may last for the night, but a shout of joy comes in the morning.
>
> —PSALM 30:5, NASB

> The Lord will comfort Israel again and make her deserts blossom. Her barren wilderness will become as beautiful as Eden—the garden of the LORD. Joy and gladness will be found there. Lovely songs of thanksgiving will fill the air.
>
> —ISAIAH 51:3, NLT

I know a little of what it means to cling to the Lord in a time of grief. A decade or so ago, I lost six babies through repeated miscarriages. After my second miscarriage, I wept bitterly before the Lord, feeling abandoned by Him. I knew the truth of "I will never leave you or forsake you," but grief and pain shouted louder than the quiet voice of truth in that moment. In the hospital, I looked out over a small bit of wasteland where a few strands of straggly grass grew. I yelled at the grass for growing so well in such harsh conditions. I argued with the Lord as to why He made grass so sturdy and babies so fragile. He seemed distant and silent.

I did not open my Bible for a few days, and my only prayers were tears and groans. After about five days, I knew that no matter what had happened and how angry I was, I didn't know how to live without God's Word in my life. I opened up the Bible, and when I looked down at the page, it appeared to be blank except for a few verses that jumped out at me from the middle of the page.

> As a mother comforts her child, so I will comfort you...your heart will rejoice and you will flourish like grass.
>
> —ISAIAH 66:13–14, NIV

I knew without a shadow of a doubt at that moment that the Lord was not only comforting me but also promising us another baby. The four subsequent losses did not shake the comfort and reassurance received that day: God was with me, and He knew what He was doing. I tasted the bitter waters of grief and waded through it, but it did not make me bitter inside. I started a prayer group for mothers in this position, and one by one each of them became pregnant, left the group and produced healthy babies. Two years later, after a troublesome and uncertain pregnancy, we too held our promised child in our arms. The Lord had added much more to our family than a child; He also added new depths of compassion and understanding.

The Lord can transform any grief into joy and teach us much in the process if we allow Him. Not everyone does—some refuse His comfort and allow a spirit of grief to overshadow them for the rest of their lives, keeping them forever wandering in the desert.

MAHLAH AND INTERCESSION

Mahlah. Her name seems to carry such burdens, doesn't it? But there is good news! This name, best revealed in the spelling *Machalah*, also contains a word for beseeching prayer, *Chalah*. Mahlahs may seem outwardly to be weaklings, but scratch beneath the surface, and they are women of effective prayer!

Mahlah, now an adult, knelt on a cushion and bowed her head reverentially. Alone in the tent, she knew she had to pray. She started with some of the "fashionable" prayers that were going about, but the words seemed to stick to her palette. Choking back the tears, she rose to her feet, tossed the pillow hard into a corner and poured out a torrent of words from her heart.

"God, I miss my dad! I miss his stories and his laughter and…and I'm angry he didn't have a son." She wiped away tears of pain and frustration. "Lord, his name! It grieves me that he will not be remembered. It seems so unfair! He was a good man."

Alone and uninhibited, Mahlah poured out her frustration and anger—anger over her weak condition, anger over losing her dad, anger over people like Korah who caused so much trouble.

Eventually a quietness descended upon her. She felt as if someone had picked her up and carried her on silken wings. Her mind was clear and at peace, and she knew that whatever had just taken place, she had forgiven her dad for leaving her with no brothers, forgiven Korah for stirring up so much trouble and forgiven God for making her a weakling. As she wept and prayed, a thought had been placed quietly in her mind, a thought so radical that it should have scared her, but the quietness in her spirit was profound, and there was no fear in her heart.

Weakness, illness and grief should drive us to our knees, as we saw earlier with Goshen's groans. I have a few good prayers for these times: "Oh, God!" and "Jesus!" Sometimes they are extended to "Oh, God, I can't bear it! Help me!" Our prayers do not have to be long-winded and complicated to be effective. Sometimes it is hard to articulate even the smallest prayer when we are in the thick of things, but most can manage a groan. Hannah groaned from her heart and emerged from her labor with the prophetic promise of a son, Samuel, who would grow to become a mighty man of God.

The Holy Spirit is the best trainer in intercession, tailor-making prayer courses perfectly fit for us and our circumstances at the time. If Mahlah reminds us that weakness can turn to strength through prayer, the Holy Spirit is the One who helps us get there. I imagine Him as a gentle dove with huge, sparkling, white wings spanning from heaven to earth. One wing touches the heart of the Father, and the other touches our hearts as He stands in the gap, interceding for us. Embraced by His wing tip, He trains our arms for battle, teaching us what to pray for and how to pray. (See Romans 8:26.)

MACHALAH AND THE CHALLAH BREAD

Mahlah arose early and had not only collected the manna, but also baked the bread from it before the others even stirred. As she ground the coriander-like substance and added oil to make it into dough, she continued to pray. Her heart was still in grief, but it had lost its bitter edge. Something had changed inside her, and making bread this morning gave her time to reflect on happy memories and on the goodness of God.

Chalah is not only intercession. It is also a type of bread or cake. Challah bread was well oiled, pierced and striped, used in the sacrifice of thanksgiving as a first-fruits bread. (See Leviticus 7:12.) To this day, for the Sabbath and special occasions, Jewish people bake it as a reminder of the manna that fell from the heavens.

It was challah bread that David gave out in "party bags" to everyone who attended the festivities of the return of the ark. This was David's way of saying, "Let's celebrate and give thanks to the Lord for His goodness to us!" He also distributed flagons of wine, pointing prophetically to the Last Supper when Jesus took wine and challah bread and served it to His disciples.

Challah bread is not for those who are desert defeatists. It is the food for overcomers.

MAHLAH

> To him who overcomes, I will give some of the hidden
> manna. I will also give him a white stone with a new
> name written on it, known only to him who receives it.
> —REVELATION 2:17, NIV

We might think it's not worth overcoming whatever we
are facing just for a slice of bread! But this is special food
sent from heaven. It is the hidden manna that was once
locked up but later released in Jesus, the Bread of Life, and
along with it comes a stone with a name etched on it. (In
ancient judiciary courts, the guilty were given a black stone
while the acquitted were given white.) God enjoys names!
The name written on this acquittal stone is not a name
change which anyone and everyone would know and use. It
is more a name of affection and intimacy, such as the name
a husband might call his wife—something special, known
only to them.

The Jews have a "hidden bread," which they conceal
during the Passover ceremony. Traditionally, there is always
a little available during the year for anyone who has a need
for healing.

The stone and the bread represent forgiveness and life
and, overall, an intimate relationship with God. It is worth
overcoming any desert experience for that! Bread, manna or
challah—call it what we may—it is survival food for those
pressing through the desert.

MAHLAH AND FORGIVENESS

So the second part of Mahlah's name, *Challah,* reminds us of
bread, Jesus and intercession. The first part of her name,
machal, makes the connection between bread and forgiveness,
for (yes—you guessed it!) *machal* means "forgive."

The Jews have three words for forgiveness: *mechila,*
selicha and *kappara.*[1]

If we imagine an offence being written on a slate, *mechila*
crosses it out with the words "paid in full," *selicha* crosses it

out but does so with empathy and understanding, *kappara* (atonement) crosses it out, understands and then wipes the slate totally clean.

Forgiveness is fundamental for getting from our desert season, where many hurts occur and are resolved, to our destiny. It is about releasing debts. When a sin is committed against us, when we are misjudged, hurt, accused or violated in some way, then a debt is incurred. We all know that and have probably cried out, "But it's wrong, and someone has to pay for it! Otherwise, it's not fair!"

Well, the truth is, no matter what the sin, Jesus has paid for it already. The debt is cancelled in full because He died for them as well as for us. To think otherwise is to diminish the power of the cross. If Jesus has paid the debt, then it's done, over, finito!

If we hold onto that debt then we end up paying a price for that "luxury" and, while the person who hurts us may walk off free, we are left ensnared ourselves. It is much easier on ourselves in the long run to literally allow Jesus to "cross out" the debt.

So what about the difference between all the types of forgiveness, does that apply to us too? Are we called to forgive and forget, as God does when He atones? Well, even after we have drawn the cross over a debt, it may take some time for the slate to be wiped clean. It might fade over time or might have to wait until heaven for a complete erasing. But the debt has still been paid, and we will know when we have released that debt when resentment and bitterness no longer eat at us and we can truly bless the one who hurt us.

Forgiveness is an art, learned only through difficult situations. The tougher the situation, the more valuable artwork is produced in the end! And the more insults that come our way, the more opportunities we have to release the power of the cross into the lives of those around us—and even into our own.

You might be saying, "You don't know what happened to

me, it's impossible for me to forgive!" I don't know, but God does, and with Him nothing is impossible.

"The things which are impossible with men are possible with God" (Luke 18:27).

FORGIVENESS AND RECIRCLING

Hebrew is a fascinating language that weaves rich threads of meaning—the word *Mechila* also means "a dance or a circle." That is not as far away from the meaning of forgiveness as it might look at first. Forgiveness completes the circle that has been broken through sin, hurt and pain. Releasing forgiveness to others turns the jagged edges of our lives (and theirs) into even circles, making lives and relationships roll more smoothly.

Circle dances are a lovely picture of this. Usually in these dances you must hold the hands of the person on either side of you. Standing side by side, hand in hand, is very hard to do if forgiveness has not been offered—and received.

There is a circle dance mentioned in the Bible, the dance of Mahanaim, between the lover and his bride. (See Song of Songs 6:13.) Mahanaim is the place Jacob called the "camp of God" where he met with God and prepared for reconciliation with his brother. (See Genesis 32:1.) When God's camp and ours connect, when our tents are joined, we do the dance of Mahanaim. This bridal dance has graceful steps—forgiveness and ardent love, reconciliation and peace. Every time we forgive someone else or receive the Lord's forgiveness for ourselves, we replace our own pain with poise and can dance these steps with joy.

MACHALAH THE NACHALAH

Sickness, weakness, grief, intercession, bread, forgiveness, circles, dancing? Mahlah's prophetically loaded name points us to Jesus and to the cross.

He was despised and rejected by men, a man of *sorrows*, and familiar with *suffering*...Surely he took up our *infirmities* and carried our sorrows, yet we considered him stricken by God, smitten by him, and *afflicted*. But he was pierced for our transgressions, he was *crushed* for our iniquities; the punishment that brought us peace was upon him, and *by his stripes we are healed*.

—ISAIAH 53:3–5, NIV, EMPHASIS ADDED

Mahlah's name has one more interesting and light-hearted twist. It rhymes with *nachalah*, the Hebrew word for "inheritance." I can imagine that Mahlah at some point was called "Machalah, the Nachalah," the diseased one who received her inheritance.

Mahlah. Her name is rich with meaning for those who, against all odds, press through their desert times and lay hold of their inheritance in Christ.

"Come on, my Mahlah," urged her mother, *"you can do it! Walk to Papa!"* Mahlah had taken her first steps that morning, and Zelophehad had missed seeing them. When he came home, his wife tried unsuccessfully to coax the toddler to take another step. Zelophehad was more patient.

"She'll move when she's ready," he said, picking her up and taking her outside the tent. Placing his daughter a few feet away, he knelt down in the sand and beckoned her with outstretched arms. Grinning from ear to ear, Mahlah stumbled forward and took three clumsy steps before lurching, gurgling, into the safety of her father's arms. *"Yes, this one will go a long way,"* Zelophehad thought to himself, *"in spite of her weakness."*

CHAPTER 5

Noah

M rs. Zelophehad soon recognized her second baby was different—a restless little bundle, even in the womb. Where Mahlah had grown quietly, this one was energetic and always on the move, just like the community she would be born into. Mrs. Zelophehad longed for rest from her wanderings. Living in a tent was no picnic at the best of times, but during pregnancy it was much harder. No matter how many times Zelophehad, as a doting husband, urged his beloved to sit down and relax, she could never quite get comfortable. The Pregnant Women's Club regularly gave talks on "Expecting Bumps on the Road," but they didn't make the journey any easier.

One evening, after a long day of setting up camp, Mrs. Zelophehad flopped onto her mat ready for a good night's sleep. Nestling into a curve in the sand beneath her, she felt a sharp pain in her side and winced. She was tired but had not lost her sense of humor. She rolled over, lifted the corner of the *mat and gave a wry grin to her husband. He reached over and pried a small rock from the hardened sand.*

"If this is a boy," she announced emphatically, "I am going to call him Noah. Then, at last, I'll get comfortable!"

Zelophehad was well aware that the name meant "rest and comfort." "Not that Noah got much rest," he chuckled, "building a floating zoo is a lot of hard work and splinters. And then there was all that tossing and turning on the waves!" He dramatically tossed the culprit rock out of his tent.

His wife still had to contend with her baby who jostled within, arms and legs competing for space. "Well, at least Noah got his rest in the end," she muttered. "Goodnight, my little Noah." Mrs. Zelophehad patted the child in her womb and drifted off to sleep, dreaming of snow-white doves, rainbow-colored mountains and a place to call home.

Zelophehad took longer to fall sleep. He was pondering this whole naming business. "Noah," he eventually concluded, "will be an excellent name!"

NOAH, LITTLE MISS MOTION

Noah. The name floods the mind with pictures of boats and animals, but the only ark Zelophehad's second child would know was the ark of the covenant. And this was to become no white-bearded sailor—this Noah was a girl.

Like her namesake, she was a survivor, but they survived very different situations; one Noah survived a flood, the other a desert. Their names are similarly extreme in meaning: Noah, the girl's name, is the flip side of the coin to Mr. Noah Ark. The female version means "moving in an agitated manner" and "wandering" whereas the male Noah means "rest and comfort." Another difference in the male name is its pronunciation, which is "Noach" (with a gutteral *ch*).

So what led Mr. and Mrs. Zelophehad to call their second daughter Noah? It is hardly more appealing than Mahlah, at face value. Why did this young couple not pick sweet names meaning flower, peace or mercy? The answer might well lie in the circumstances of their lives. The root of Noah, *nuwa*, gives us a clue. Since the Bible uses *nuwa* to describe the wanderings in the desert, it seems likely that she was named Noah because she was to be another "little wanderer." (See Numbers 32:13.)

DESERT VAGRANTS

Nuwa is not a relaxed peaceful meander. Looking more closely, we see it means "to tremble or shake, be sifted or tossed about." It can also mean "to wander, waver or stagger in an agitated manner." This name makes me think of a drunken vagrant staggering through a dark city, unable to ever find comfort and rest. In fact this root, as a noun, can be translated "vagrant." Imagine having a little girl who lived up to a name like that!

A vagrant is someone who has no home and is often in this sad condition because life has treated him badly. Abuse, either from his own hands or the hands of others, has pushed him into living a life of misery—wandering around in the desert with no purpose instead of living in a rich community full of hope and promise.

While our desert may not be caused by drunkenness and abuse, we can still be in dry times that make us feel we are wandering about and getting nowhere. They are unstable times, when we feel shaky and stagger around unsure of where we are headed. We know we're supposed to be going places, but we're not sure when and where or how!

Desert times can break a person. Or they can transform the wanderer into one who knows how to move through life with direction, purpose and poise.

Little Noah Motion was born with a destiny, just as we are. But before she could take hold of that, she had to learn how to make the *right* moves. How she would choose to move would either keep her in the desert or allow her to take her destiny.

WRESTLING WITH OUR TREMBLES

Noah was really a "chip off the old block," which is a British expression meaning she was like her dad. Both Zelophehad's name and that of his daughter have a connection to trembling.

How many people that we have met have a tendency to say, "I can't do it" or "I could never do that—I am much too nervous"? I have led various women's ministries over the years and love to stretch the ladies beyond what they have previously done. It might seem like a small step to some, but for others to pray out loud, lead a Bible study or share their opinion seems just too much and they respond, "Oh, I wish I could, but even the thought of it makes me want to run away!"

I've had my share of fearful moments, but have learned not to let my trembling hold me back. Trembling demonstrates our weakness and highlights God's strength. The Lord often chooses to use those who consider themselves weak rather than those who think themselves—and indeed even are—strong or fit for the job.

I've already told you about my fear of insects and spiritual warfare, but I also feared speaking in public. Doing anything up front often made me shake, rattle and roll right out of the room! At school, I was anxious about reading out loud and devised ways to get out of it, including ducking under the seat to retrieve something when my turn was coming up. As a teenager, I was a member of a simple music group, Illumination, that played in a variety of low-key locations. I had so many internal butterflies seeking to overwhelm me, I referred to the group as Elimination; before playing I was almost always a nervous mess. I used to dread doing the Bible reading in church; after all, how could I read from a

Bible that was shaking so much the words were blurred?

I was fortunate to have people around me who ignored my pleas to let me sit back. They coaxed, prodded and pushed me, and wiped away my tears of frustration, pushing me out past the barriers I had set myself. I memorized verses like the following to encourage myself to "give things a go" in spite of my fears:

> Hear, O Israel, you are approaching the battle against your enemies today. Do not be fainthearted. Do not be afraid, or panic, or tremble before them.
> —DEUTERONOMY 20:3, NASB

> Be strong and courageous, do not be afraid or tremble at them, for the LORD your God is the one who goes with you. He will not fail you or forsake you.
> —DEUTERONOMY 31:6, NASB

> I can do all things through Christ who strengthens me.
> —PHILIPPIANS 4:13, NKJV

Frankly, my shakes did not always stop. And I would get mad at God for what seemed to me to be not keeping His side of the bargain. But somehow, in spite of my trembles, I managed to do the tasks in hand—and the Lord received the glory. I still shake sometimes when asked to do certain things but won't let nerves stop me from doing something I know the Lord is asking of me; the fear of refusing Him is stronger than the fear of looking foolish.

Trembling is not always a negative thing, as we saw with fear in a previous chapter. We are told to work out our own salvation "with fear and trembling" (Phil. 2:12). What does that mean? Are we not supposed to enjoy God's love rather than shake in His presence? Fortunately, the two are not mutually exclusive.

In the middle of an injunction to encourage each other, Paul throws in a profound description of Jesus becoming a man and dying on the cross. The thought of almighty God doing such an act of humility and love should cause us to tremble and ask, "How can it be that God loves me so much?" What a God! Such a revelation of *His* love should make the practice of working out our salvation, loving one another, all the more easy.

So is the Christian walk supposed to be just one big tremble? No, this is one of the many biblical paradoxes: it is good for us to know how to tremble, in the right way and for the right reasons, but we must also be still and rest. And, believe it or not, we can do both at the same time.

Wrestling and Resting

Noah, Mr. Ark, knew how to tremble appropriately: to wrestle as well as rest. Remember he sent out the dove three times to see if there was dry land? The first time the dove returned having found no land. Noah waited seven days before sending it out again. This time it came back with a fresh olive leaf, and Noah waited seven days again before releasing it the last time. (See Genesis 8:10.)

The word *waited* or *stayed* is *chuwl*, meaning "a trembling, restless or writhing movement," often used by intercessors to describe a time of travail. Noah didn't just hang around dealing with elephant dung while waiting for the next stage of his life to unfold; he was busy trembling before the Lord in prayer. He was resting and wrestling at the same time—resting obediently in his place in the ark but trembling in intercession for the next step for humanity to be birthed.

After our storms there are in-between times. We know things are shifting around us, and we keep sending out "doves" to see if change will happen this week! The waters from the storms of life are subsiding, but we cannot just rush out and possess the land of our promises until the Lord tells us it is time. The in-between days are days of travail—days of waiting and interceding for His purposes to come forth.

Don Stephens, director of Mercy Ships, is a modern-day Noah. He had a vision of a ship that would bring mercy and relief to thousands of people all over the world: a ship equipped as a hospital, laden with supplies, and staffed by Christians who would perform surgery and demonstrate the love of God in other practical ways.

One day Don received a fax from George Verwer, another Noah. George had already proved that penniless people could buy a ship: *Logos*, part of Operation Mobilisation, was already sailing around the world as a giant floating bookshop taking the good news and "good books for all." George had been hunting for a ship to add to his expanding ministry and called Don to say he had seen one, too large for OM's purposes, that might well suit what Don had in mind: a floating hospital!

The size of the ship and its cost, in spite of its suitability, appeared daunting, but Don declared, "It may be too big for us, but it's not too big for God."

Don, his wife, Deyon, and their friends faced many difficulties in their "in-between time," but, like Noah, they waited on the Lord, wrestling in prayer until eventually they climbed on board their new home, *Anastasis*.

Neither Don nor George allowed their trembling fears about finances or the enormity of the vision to hold them back from the visions God had given them. Operation Mobilisation now sails two ships, and Mercy Ships sails three, all five training thousands of young people to have a heart for missions while reaching into the most needy nations of the world.

MOVERS AND SHAKERS

One way to get rid of unhelpful trembles is to replace them with a good old shake of faith! One of the first things the Lord did for His people as He led them into the desert was to shake off the Egyptians. (See Exodus 14:27.)

This shaking process reminds me of when I lived in Borneo and brought dry washing in from the line. Before folding the laundry, we had to shake it vigorously to get rid of any lingering bugs.

The desert is a place where we can feel we have been washed up, wrung out and then put on a line in the baking sun to dry. And then, just when we think we are about to be taken down and used again in some way, along comes God with a giant shaking hand! It might not feel very good, but this is a worthwhile shake that shows progress is being made and God is getting ready to use us in fresh ways.

Sometimes He does the shaking for us. At other times He expects us to shake off "Egypt" ourselves.

> Shake off your dust; rise up, sit enthroned, O Jerusalem. Free yourself from the chains on your neck, O captive Daughter of Zion.
>
> —ISAIAH 52:2, NIV

A major component of dust is dead skin cells. Who wants yesterday's dead skin hanging around? And, as if it's bad enough having to deal with our own dead skins cells, remember that dust contains everyone else's dead bits too. If we learn to shake off the dead stuff that clings to us, we will get through our desert seasons much faster.

I asked my daughter's friend, Sarah, age nineteen, if she had ever done a shake like this. She responded, with appropriate shaking gestures of her arms, "Oh, yes, sometimes I have thoughts racing inside my head telling me that I cannot do something, whispering what people think of me. I have to shake them off by remembering what the Lord has said about who I am." Sarah has learned an important lesson early in life that will stand her in good stead. Noah was probably a teenager when she learned this too.

Noah. She rose above the labels put on her by her name and refused to let her fears hold her back from God's best for her. She did not listen to the voices either within or without that said, "I can't do it. It's too costly. It's too scary." She stepped out, perhaps shaking in her boots, and reached for her inheritance. Noah defeated the negatives in her name, building them instead into positive attributes. Instead of a shaking one, she turned out to be a true mover and shaker.

This makes me think of the Shaker Movement, known for its quakes, shakes and ecstatic dances. These dances were meant to shake off the enemy and his devices. While dancing may sometimes be a good way to resist the enemy, we don't have to work ourselves up into a frenzy to do so. But we do need to raise up a generation of movers and shakers that have allowed themselves to be transformed by the Lord and will go out and shake their nations. Transformed young Noahs make a difference; they make things happen.

SHAKING WITH THE STRENGTH OF A LION

You might say you do not have the strength to be a mover and a shaker. Well, our shaking is never about how strong we are, but rather how strong the Lord is. "I can't" is desert language whereas "God can" is in the phrase book of inheritors.

This is brought out beautifully in another word for *shake*, *na'ar*. This is a vigorous, purposeful shake that demonstrates power, like a lion shaking its mane. It is the shaking of strength—His, not our own. We, even in our weakness, are called to be like the Lion of Judah. We have His Spirit within us, and we must allow His godly roar to rise up, shake the weights off our backs and give us freedom to *move*!

Mary, an intercessor, came to me and asked me to pray for her. For twenty years she had been praying for the gift of tongues, the ability to speak and pray in a language she had not learned. She knew its importance, wanted it badly and had been faithful in asking for it. Many times Mary went forward at meetings and asked people for prayer or advice. I wondered what I could possibly add that would make a difference. I decided to stall for time (so I could pray!) and sent her away to ask the Lord one more time on her own. She came back the next day with no progress and a heavy heart. Something inside me made me mad that she had been kept so long from opening up the gift the Lord was offering to her. To my surprise, I found myself telling her firmly, "Mary, I'm not going to pray for you. You do not need any more prayer. You need to get angry. Get angry with the enemy. Tell him who comes to kill, steal and destroy that you will not be stolen from for one more day!" She looked a bit stunned for a second or two and then slowly nodded.

Within the day Mary was not only speaking but also singing beautifully in tongues. She came up to me during worship, beaming, and sang the sweetest heavenly song into my ear. Mary had done a lion's shaking. She had roared "Enough!" and received another part of her inheritance.

Over what should we deliver a lion's roar? Well, what is it that the enemy has stolen from us, killed or destroyed? (See John 10:10.) Those contested areas need to be roared over because they are likely to be the very things that will help us to fulfill our personal destiny.

The same thing applies on a corporate level. I believe every Christian family has a unique purpose together, a special flavor or a particular anointing. Some have a call to hospitality, others to missions, others to evangelism. It may be a special mandate for a season, but working together they will achieve far more than if they were separate.

> Five of you will chase a hundred...and your enemies
> will fall by the sword before you.
> —LEVITICUS 26:8, NIV

Is it any wonder that the enemy tries so hard to break up, tear down and prevent families from reaching their corporate destiny? Our family has a call wrapped up in "east meets west." Some people told us before our wedding that we were crazy to consider a marriage based on such a wide cultural divide. Undaunted, we chose a hymn to sing at our wedding that would be a loud roar: "In Christ there is no east or west, in Him no north or south."[1] Our interracial marriage made us a bridge between two cultures, one small step in bringing unity to the body of Christ.

What is your family's call? And what is your family's roar? Remember, it may well lie in that most contested area!

Churches, too, can have a special call they must roar over, as have cities and nations. The city of Fremantle here in Western Australia, by virtue of its name, has a call to freedom—to wear a "free mantle." The enemy is trying to steal its freedom and replace it with New Age bondage. But the churches in Fremantle are not sitting back and letting it happen. They are giving their love to the poorest people in the city through canceling debts and other acts of loving-kindness. One day Fremantle will be free because the church has demonstrated the love of Christ and roared "Jesus is Lord!" over it often enough!

SIFTING

Nuwa can also be translated "sifting." Shaking deals with the bigger, more obvious issues. Sifting, on the other hand, takes care of the less noticeable little things that have crept into our lives.

> I will sift the house of Israel among all nations, like as corn is sifted in a sieve.
> —AMOS 9:9, KJV

God sifts us. It is another desert maneuver that removes rubbish, often unperceived at the time, from our lives.

Living in the tropics, we had to sift our flour before using it. The first few times I bought flour, I returned it because it was crawling with weevils. I soon learned that if I continued to do that, I would never do any baking—every packet was infested. We learned to keep our flour in the freezer and to sift it several times before use. The first sieving was to get the beasts out, the next to add air to the mixture. This second sifting, as all good bakers know, has to be done from a height so that the cake will rise as it should.

God sifts us from the heights of heaven to get rid of the dross that would spoil the cake He is baking in us! Depending on how many weevils are eating away at us, we may need a few sifts to enable our spirits to rise to greater heights.

How does it feel to be sifted, dropped from a height? Perhaps you were dropped from some program or role you were thoroughly enjoying. Maybe you were on the worship team one day and off the next, and you have no idea what you did wrong. Were you pastoring a church and forced to resign because they wanted someone younger? Or maybe your shattering experience has come in another painful way: rejection, lack of acknowledgment, accusations. No sooner did it seem you were flying high when you crashed to the ground. And as you go from dizzying heights to somewhere near ground level, it may feel as if lightness in your spirit is the last thing that will ever come of it. Sifting hurts, but listen, hurting hearts—it is worth it!

Parent eagles push their eaglets out from the nest to teach them how to fly. As the little ones plummet headfirst towards the ground, they have to quickly learn how to flap their wings. But the wise female bird has chosen father eagle because he is a good "catcher": during their courtship flights she dropped sticks for her suitor to demonstrate his catching ability, which he would use to rescue eaglets until they perfected their flying skills.

We may feel, in the sifting process, that we are racing headfirst into a disaster, but the Father knows what He is doing and is precise in His timing to bring us safely back up on His wings.

Two of our children, Jared and Kirstine, once had visions of replacing a grassy patch of our garden with pretty flowers full of color. I warned them they would have to get every root of grass out first, or it would come up again and choke the flowers. They rolled up their sleeves and soon had the grass and its major roots out. But then came the sifting job, separating soil from the lesser roots shovel by shovel. At the end of the day, with a big pile of roots, a smaller pile of soil and still much to do, two weary children gave up. It took Dad to come along with weed killer and a truckload of fresh soil to get rid of the offending weeds and prepare the flower bed—by then the kids had moved onto greener "pastures," and we are still waiting for the flowers!

The desert can sift and remove roots, big and small, that would choke us—roots of bitterness and unforgiveness, selfishness or greed, laziness or lust. It's no good trying to plant good things alongside them, hoping they will outgrow the weeds. Every root of weed must come out first. So if you are being shifted and sifted in these areas just now, rejoice that the Master Sifter is processing the soil of your life to promote greater beauty and color!

Tossed About

Nuwa also translates "tossed about." Where shaking deals with the outer dust and sifting roots, tossing relates to doubts. It has that sense of agitated "to-ing and fro-ing" like a wave on the ocean moving backwards and forwards but never seeming to make progress. James likens tossing about to lack of faith.

> But let him ask in faith, with no doubting, for he who doubts is like a wave of the sea driven and tossed by the wind.
>
> —James 1:6

Think of Mr. Noah again. In the worst of the storms, he was in circumstances that would make most people seasick. His circumstances were outwardly turbulent, but inwardly he was not tossed about. He was at rest, as his name suggests, working away at the tasks in hand, praying and resting in a deep trust that God was in control.

What kinds of things make us toss about? Worry? Fear? Doubt? Stress? The list is long. Undoubtedly the wild seas of life will rage against us at times. Storms come—but they also go again. What we have to learn is how to stay stable in the midst of them, and faith is the key to that stability.

Jenny, a dear friend of mine, was to undergo serious and painful tests for breast cancer so I went along to help her pass the inevitable long waits between appointments. The waiting room was full of tension as each lady waited to be tested or told of test outcomes. Jenny's heart, resolutely trusting in the Lord, was moved with compassion by the fear on the other ladies' faces, even as she faced her own storm. We prayed quietly for those in the room and chatted about the Lord, while in-between times Jenny went from room to room and doctor to doctor.

Jenny finally learned she had a malignant tumor. She was told to go off, have some lunch and be back in an hour to see a surgeon. At a time when most people could not have eaten because of fear and tension, Jenny ate heartily, we talked about the Lord's goodness and we both almost forgot why we were there. At the end of the day, although very tired, Jenny told me she had had a lovely day. So had I, just being with her. What a God, who can turn darkness into joy, right there and then, even in the midst of pain and fear! Instead of being tossed about, Jenny was being moved and continues, now cancer free, to be moved by God's love and promises towards her.

WAVERING AND WANDERING

Another slant on the study of *nuwa* is "wavering" and "wandering." We all waver at times. Some people do it more than others, but we all have the tendency. Wavering means we are behaving as waves, coming and going, teetering on the brink of decision. Waverers can't make up their minds. They stagger between two opinions, of the Lord and even of themselves. One minute they are full of faith and vision, and the next they are down and out, unable to hold on to truth.

The Lord wants us to be stable in all our ways, including the way we think about ourselves. Faith and trust do not allow for wavering. Faith hears what the Lord has said about a matter and acts on it. Wavering, so often simply being at the mercy of our emotions, can leave us shipwrecked on the rocks of defeatism when the Lord simply requires, as with wandering, that we trust him.

> Let us hold fast the confession of our hope without wavering, for He who promised is faithful.
> —HEBREWS 10:23

Holding fast is the answer to wavering, and here the sense is to hold something so firmly in our minds that we own it. Wanderers are similar to waverers: aimless and indecisive.

> My brothers, if one of you should wander from the truth…
> —JAMES 5:19, NIV

> If a man owns a hundred sheep, and one of them wanders away…And if he finds it, I tell you the truth, he is happier about that one sheep than about the ninety-nine that did not wander off.
> —MATTHEW 18:12–13, NIV

> The people wander like sheep oppressed for lack of a shepherd.
> —ZECHARIAH 10:2, NIV

Wanderers have not stayed close to the Shepherd, to be fed and guided by Him. They have wandered from the truth, believing the lies that their Good Shepherd cannot take care of them or lead them safely through valleys and deserts.

The answer to wandering is relationship and trust. The

desert transforms wanderers into followers who move together as one flock under the care of their Shepherd.

The word wanderer is significant for me: one meaning of *Wendy* being "wanderer" is a good reminder for me not to wander from the Good Shepherd! I have also found a helpful way of dealing with my waverings. I remember there is more to me than my emotions, and when they are raging around me, tossing me every which way, I imagine myself reaching down into my spirit and drawing from a deep well in there. When I do that, the living water of the Lord rises up and washes over my emotions, calming them. I am drawing truth from my innermost being and using it to control my flesh and emotional whims. As my friends and family will tell you, I am no expert at this, but I am learning!

Had Noah been controlled by untrained flesh, she would never have made her journey to the tent of meeting. She was not a wanderer who accidentally chanced upon the tent of meeting and suddenly thought of something to ask for. Nor was she apologetic or wavering in the way she asked for it. Can you imagine if she had petitioned Moses, cowering at his feet, "Moses, if you're willing, may I have this land? I know I'm unworthy—after all, I'm not a man, and I don't have any rights here. But Moses, would you please consider my request and not kill me for asking?"

No, Noah's approach to Moses was a planned, deliberate action requiring attributes learned, not in an instant, but slowly, over time.

More Kingdom Moves

Many more word pictures in the Bible show us how to move in godly ways. Different moves are right for different seasons of our lives, and sometimes we can be doing more than one at once. We are called to *walk* in the light, to walk in His paths, to walk and not faint. No wandering here—these are purposeful, steady steps of obedience, taken in divine order.

NOAH

My husband, true to his Chinese roots, often tells us, "The journey of a thousand miles begins with the first step." When babies take their first few steps, they might stagger and reel, but in this case it's positive: they're driven by an inner urge to get to their destination—watch how soon they learn to make a beeline for the cookie jar! Our first spiritual steps may also be shaky, but they are a good beginning and will lead to extraordinary journeys with God, with richer rewards than cookies.

"Well," I hear you say, "I *have* been trying to walk, but I feel as if my Christian life has been one step forward, two steps back." Don't worry about that—any steps forward are worth a lot more than the backward sort, and before we know it our spiritual leg muscles are set not only to walk, but to run.

There are periods in our lives when the spiritual pace picks up. Everything is accelerated. We're on an exercise machine, and someone has cranked up the speed to a *running* pace. We are learning fast, growing rapidly, being stretched. But we are exhilarated! Running is good for us. It enlarges our hearts so we can "run upon troops" and "leap over walls." And all the time, our wonderful Coach runs out ahead, beckoning us forward.

We must just make sure that we are not trying to compete with one another or run someone else's race for them. The Lord has set a path for us for a season, and we must be obedient to run only in that lane. We must also learn to run at the Lord's pace. If we don't, we will exhaust ourselves and those around us. Running ahead of God is one certain way to breed weariness in our lives. The Lord always provides plenty of stops—times to wait, to rest on His breast and enjoy His renewing power.

> But those who wait on the LORD shall renew their strength ... they shall run and not be weary.
> —ISAIAH 40:31

Weariness is not the same thing as having a healthy

muscle ache from the new stretching exercises the Lord has given us. We will still need endurance, strength and determination for the long distance run, and we must wear the right shoes, the gospel of peace. If our running around is not based on bringing the good news to those who need it—we are wearing the wrong shoes, and all we get is blistered feet!

Correctly attired, we run as a team with no sense of competition between us, all pressing towards the same goal, to know Christ and to make Him known. And we run to win knowing we have already won, cheered on by those who have gone before. The prize will be worth it in the end!

Some days our walking and running is so filled with grace that we seem to be *dancing* along, unfazed by the storms that would otherwise toss us about. I love the famous painting, *The Singing Butler*, by Scottish artist Jack Vettriano. It shows an elegant couple in evening attire dancing on the beach, servants doing battle to shield them with umbrellas against howling wind and driving rain. The servants are bothered by the weather, but the couple are so engrossed in each other that they dance on, blissfully unaware. If we are engrossed in Jesus, dancing in His arms, then the storms of life that blow our way will have a far less devastating effect on us.

MOVING LIPS

Having said that, there are times when we feel we just cannot raise a foot to walk, let alone dance or run. Life bears down on us too heavy and too hard. That's OK! Nuwa teaches us one more good move: "moving lips."

> Hannah was praying in her heart, and her lips were moving [*nuwa*] but her voice was not heard.
> —1 SAMUEL 1:13, NIV

Hannah's inner groan was a *nuwa* prayer, said with shaking body and trembling lips, but it brought her into her destiny as the mother of a great prophet. Her desert of barrenness became a place of promise.

Are you feeling barren? Do you have a longing to birth something? Have you been taunted and abused because you haven't managed so far? Take it to the Lord in prayer! Our prayers don't have to be fancy. Even if our lips tremble, our face is a mess, we resemble a drunken woman and people misunderstand us, God is listening and setting things into motion around us. Even if our words seem incoherent to others, He hears our heart!

Fortunately, our prayer times are not always shaky ones. There are times when moving our lips in prayer is much easier! They are times when the Lord will ask us to hover over situations in a type of intercession that is as easy and relaxed as an albatross hovering over the ocean.

Hovering with God

God does not ask us to do anything He is not willing to do Himself, and He demonstrates the moves He asks us to make. Hovering was the first movement mentioned in the Bible; it is in the context of dark and deep waters being transformed into light.

> The earth was empty, a formless mass cloaked in darkness. And the Spirit of God was hovering over its surface. Then God said, "Let there be light," and there was light.
>
> —Genesis 1:2–3, NLT

Hovering in this verse is a soft, relaxed movement of the Spirit's wings. The picture contained in the word is of a gentle fluttering or rippling movement as the wings gracefully extend out to brood over the dark waters. Where there is brooding, there is birth. In this verse, it was the birth of light upon the earth. But the Lord didn't stop hovering once light was established. Next time we see the Word, we are told

He is hovering over His people—in the desert!

> He found him [the tribes of Jacob] in a desert land
> and in the wasteland, a howling wilderness; He encir-
> cled him, He instructed him, He kept him as the apple
> of His eye. As an eagle stirs up its nest, hovers over its
> young, spreading out its wings, taking them up, car-
> rying on its wings, so the LORD alone led him.
> —DEUTERONOMY 32:10–12

It is encouraging to know that we are not the only ones moving. God moves behind us, before us and above us! He is encircling, watching and hovering over His people until they learn to soar themselves.

And we will! The desert trains us to brood and hover, taught by the Great Trainer in Intercession, the Holy Spirit. As we extend our "wings" of prayer in a relaxed and confident manner over darkness situations, we will see them transformed by the light of God.

Our young son, one day, saw an open vision, rather like a movie screen before his eyes. He saw an angel flying through the sky over a pathway to heaven's gates. The angel held a dove's nest in his hands and as he flew he dropped soft, white feathers into the air. These feathers hovered in the air and slowly drifted to earth. When they touched the soil, they burst into large feather plants. One feather of the Holy Dove is enough to explode with fruitfulness into feather plants. It is in His nature to be fruitful. When we learn to move our lips and hover in intercession, we can be certain it will bear much fruit.

THE SIGNALS TO MOVE

We talked a little earlier about moving in the right lanes and waiting on God. We have to discern when He is moving and follow. Moses knew about this. He was not prepared to take one step without the Lord.

Then Moses said, "If you don't go with us personally, don't let us move a step from this place."
—EXODUS 33:15, NLT

The whole time His people were in the desert, He made sure someone had their eyes on the cloud! And the lesson was one of obedience. Stay when God says stay, and move when God says move:

When you sound the signal to move on, the tribes on the east side of the Tabernacle will break camp and move forward.
—NUMBERS 10:5, NLT

And it was not just walking feet that God wanted, He wanted their hearts to be moved by His love.

Now Israel, what does the Lord your God require from you, but…to walk in all His ways and love Him, and to serve the Lord your God with all your heart.
—DEUTERONOMY 10:12, NASB

Are we seeing or hearing God's signals to move on? To break away from the old camps? Cross a river to a promised land? You might say it was easy for the Israelites to know when the Lord wanted them to move on in their journey, but how can we when we don't have the reality of clouds in the sky or fire at night?

We still have signals; we just need to know how to see or hear them. We are not disadvantaged, because we see with our spiritual rather than natural eyes. In fact, being this side of the cross is a tremendous blessing! God signals to us through His Word, in our prayer closets, through our counselors and friends. Anyway, we are not left without a cloud or a fire. Our guide, the Holy Spirit, is the most gigantic glory cloud and biggest fire we could imagine! And He distributes gifts to the body of Christ that help in this signaling process: wisdom, discernment, prophecy and words of knowledge. We all have access to these in some measure, but

He also gives a special measure to apostles, prophets, pastors, teachers and evangelists to lead in a corporate way. These are the ones who will probably first hear the whistle of God when He says, "Time to move on, church!" Yes, God whistles!

> He will lift up a banner to the nations from afar, and will whistle to them from the end of the earth; surely they shall come with speed, swiftly.
> —ISAIAH 5:26

> I will whistle for them and gather them, for I will redeem them; and they shall increase as they once increased.
> —ZECHARIAH 10:8

> And it shall come to pass that in that day the Lord will whistle for the fly that is in the remotest part of the rivers of Egypt and for the bee that is in the land of Assyria.
> —ISAIAH 7:18

The Lord whistles to mobilize flies and bees, which drive the enemy out of the land. Why flies? Isn't Satan—Beelzebub—lord of the flies? Yes, but the Lord can use whom He likes, evil or good, to prepare the way for His people to take their inheritance. That is why, when bad things happen to us or to our nations, even evil things, properly understood, they can be vehicles to our destiny.

But it's not only flies He uses. He also uses bees. The Hebrew word for bee is *debash*, the same word used in the name Deborah. Deborah, of course, was a strong and prophetic signalwoman for the Lord. This little *debash* bee is not the queen bee variety, which lies around expecting everyone else to do the work while she pops eggs. The *debash* bee is a solitary bee found in the cleft of rocks. Those with a Deborah anointing will be more at home in the cleft of the rock. They may well have been hidden there for a time, but even in that place they will have left their sweetness.

Remember, you cannot have a land of milk and honey without bees!

So the Lord whistles, and His anointed bees come forth and prophetically clear the land. Men and women with a Deborah anointing may have a sting in their tail directed at the enemy, but they leave a trail of loving sweetness behind them.

I have been in many prayer meetings with mighty warring Deborahs. One I know wars with tenacious ferocity in the Spirit, but when the intercession is over she is the sweetest, mildest woman you could ever meet.

The Lord is raising up many women with this land-clearing, signalling anointing. Many have been hidden in the Cleft of the Rock, but when the Lord whistles, a huge army of them will be ready to move forward. They may have been weak Mahlahs or restless Noahs initially, but now their prayers and prophecies can be heard buzzing all the way up to heaven, and change is in the air. Put a lot of Deborahs together in one room and hear the buzz!

The Transformations II video (accounts of how unified prayer has changed nations) talks of intercession sounding like buzzing bees.[2] Once at a large women's prayer gathering, I prophesied about the rise of the Deborah bee anointing. Later a friend nudged me and asked, "Wendy, can you hear the bees?" I could—and it sounded like an advancing swarm!

Noah. When the signal blew, she recognized it and rose to her feet. She moved with courage, and she moved with wisdom. She moved at the right time towards the right place with the right attitude. And on that day, Noah ensured she would be remembered not as a wavering woman but as a daughter with a destiny of far-reaching consequences, both for herself and for society, for generations to come.

CHAPTER 6

Hoglah

---

*Z*elophehad had a problem on his hands. His young wife's belly was swelling again, and with this came some peculiar cravings. With Mahlah and Noah, she had craved comfort. This time the dear lady was permanently hungry with voracious longings for strange foods.

The men thought they'd had it bad in the desert with their meat cravings, but the Expectant Women's club had lists the length of their arms with the things they yearned for. It wasn't as if Zelophehad had a 24-hour store to run to when his wife put in an order. Even if there had been, he probably wouldn't have found her request anyway.

"Yesterday she longed for something sweet, like sugared snails," he joked with his friends, "tomorrow she'll probably want something like salted prunes!" Zelophehad's friends roared with laughter as he continued. "And today, she was fed up with manna and wanted to bake a partridge pie. I tell you, there isn't

a night when she doesn't dream of throwing a sumptuous feast!"
Little did Mrs. Zelo, or anyone else, know at the time that she
had a little "partridge" developing within her, a partridge who
would grow up to feast on the goodness of the Lord.

LITTLE MISS PARTRIDGE

Can you picture Zelophehad's third baby daughter arriving
in a tent to join one sister who was weak and another always
on the go? The new little one was promptly named *Hoglah*,
also spelled *Choglah*, which means "partridge."[1] When I first
read this, I wondered yet again at Zelophehad's choice of
name. After all, the partridge is not mentioned in the desert
account, but its close relative the quail is, several times.
Zelophehad might have thought to himself when Hoglah
was born, "This one is so like a little bird, but bigger, bonnier
and louder than a quail, so I'll upgrade her to a partridge!"

I imagine this baby was born a plump wee thing, already
bubbling with a happy spirit. I picture Hoglah growing into
a chubby, contented girl, saying to her father, "Tell me the
stories about the birds again, Papa!"

Zelophehad would settle himself down, lift little Hoglah
onto his knee and tell her the story of the Days of Quail. "It
all started, my little Hoglah, a long time ago, when the
people complained ..."

THE DAYS OF QUAIL

A lot of complaining took place in the desert. Complaints can
open doors better left shut. Much of the desert experience was
centered on ridding the Israelites of a deep-rooted grumbling
spirit; half the protests were about leadership issues, and the
rest were about food, drink or comforts of other kinds.

Food complaints started in Eden and continued to multiply until they affected an entire nation. For the Israelites in

the desert there were at least six national food grievances:

- We want water.
- We want bread and meat.
- We want more water.
- We want meat—and veggies.
- We want fruit—and water.
- We want better bread—and more water.

These people sounded like a stuck record—stuck on hidden agendas, including undermining their leadership. Food and leadership complaints frequently go together. Adam's complaint about the fruit, for example, was not so much about food but authority. While Korah attacked leadership, his cronies attacked the menu.

WATER! BREAD! MEAT!

So how did the Lord deal with these complaining people? With the first bout they received the water they asked for, in the spirit of their asking.

> When they came to Marah, they could not drink its water because it was bitter. (That is why the place is called Marah.) So the people grumbled against Moses, saying, "What are we to drink?"
> —EXODUS 15:23–24, NIV

A bitter attitude brought them to bitter water, turned sweet only by the Lord's intervention. It's a shame they didn't hang on and trust the Lord because just around the corner from Marah was what they longed for: Elim, an oasis with twelve springs, one for each tribe. Plenty of sweet water for everyone!

Next they craved bread and meat, so God sent manna and quail, and they ate well. (See Numbers 16:8–15.) God was there. God heard. God answered. In spite of their bad attitude, they seemed to get what they wanted.

MORE WATER!

The next stop for the people was Rephidim, "place of rest and refreshment." (See Exodus 17:1.) Here the people again pestered Moses to give them water. In a way it was understandable: they had walked a long way. But the Lord was hardly likely to let His people die of thirst! At His instruction, Moses struck the rock of Horeb (meaning "desert"), and water gushed forth. The desert rock became what the Lord had intended all along, a place of life-giving water. But because of the people's attitudes, Rephidim was renamed *Massah* and *Meribah*, "the place of temptation and strife."

MEAT AND VEGGIES—AND MORE WATER!

During a long stop at Sinai, where Moses received the Law, an apparently satisfied people "shared a meal in God's presence" (Exod. 24:11, NLT). But "Time to Rumble, Time to Grumble" might have been a good slogan for the Israelites. Now, over a year into their journey, the cloud moved on, and with it a discontented people. After only three days' travel, rumbling stomachs brought on the grumbling again.

Complaints are like elastic: easily stretched. Now, tired of manna, the people wanted meat for pot roasts, but also wailed to God for the taste of fish, leeks, melons, onions, garlic and cucumbers they had left behind in Egypt. (See Numbers 11:5.)

They remembered this as "free" food, forgetting the price they had paid for it was beatings, bondage and brick ovens, forgetting that much of it produced bad breath and wind. Worse still, fish, onions and leeks were considered gods in Egypt.

The Lord, in His grace, sent two winds of His Spirit bringing two types of meat: Spirit and flesh. The first wind blew on seventy men—the first Sanhedrin—and left them with a prophetic anointing. (I would love to know what they prophesied that day. Did their words include warnings about eating quail?) The second wind blew in thousands of quail. But provision this time—albeit minus the veggies— came with discipline.

On the first quail day, early in the desert, God demonstrated to the hungry people His provision and tolerance, but now after being this long in the desert, the people should have known better. The lessons about faith versus flesh had not sunk in, so He repeated the lesson. This second day of quail had more serious consequences; some of the finest, strongest men died and were buried in the Place of Craving. (See Psalm 78:31.)

> So that place was called Kibroth-hattaavah—"the graves of craving"—because they buried the people there who had craved meat from Egypt.
> —NUMBERS 11:34, NLT

WE WANT DESSERT! AND MORE WATER!

The people moved on to the Desert of Zin, where Miriam died. Perhaps it was their grief that stirred up the old complaining spirit again. With no water for the congregation, they gathered together against Moses and Aaron, accusing Moses:

> If only we had died when our brethren died before the LORD! Why have you brought up the assembly of the LORD into this wilderness, that we and our animals should die here?
> —NUMBERS 20:2–4

And they wanted more than water: almost a generation before, Joshua and Caleb had returned from the Promised Land with grapes, pomegranates and figs, and now the people were also demanding dessert—the very fruit the spies had shown was in plenty supply!

At Meribaha-Kadesh the Lord, in answer to request for advice, quietly told Moses to speak to the rock to release a flow of water. But Moses, fed up with this tiresome people he was responsible for, at the last moment lost it and struck the rock with his rod. This single act of disobedience lost the great leader his entry visa for the Promised Land.

MISERABLE MANNA! MORE WATER!

The last complaint about food came after the death of Aaron and in the middle of another move. The long journey around the Red Sea was making the people tired. (See Numbers 21:5–6.) Their daily bread, the food of the angels, they dubbed "miserable manna," and they cried out for more water. This time their complaint opened a big door of trouble—a camp overrun by biting snakes. Before they realized and repented of their sin, many died of snake poison.

The seventy prophets were perhaps not hearing well for they, of all people, should have known God had provisions for their thirst up ahead. Around the corner, just as at Elim, the Lord was leading them to watery, luxuriant places (Num. 21:10–20):

- Oboth—waterskins or bottles
- Iye abarim—place of crossing over (often a river)
- Zered—luxuriant growth
- Arnon—roaring stream
- Beer—well

If only they could have held on in faith a while longer! God was still guiding and leading, caring for and protecting His people. But they were too blind and impatient to see it.

OUR COMPLAINTS

Our churches are all too often riddled with similar complaints—sermons (the main diet for so many) are too long or short, too radical or "seeker friendly." We expect our preachers to be professional "hunter-gatherers" on our behalf, and we come up with all sorts of excuses for not collecting our own manna. No wonder much of the church is still in the desert!

During times of inner hunger, the Lord has food for us— answers, just around the corner. If only we would bite our tongues first and wait, trusting the Lord will not let us lack any good thing. At other times, the very thing we yearn for, like the fruit of the land, we could have had long before, had we only focused on the Lord instead of giants.

Perhaps we can see where "Time to Rumble, Time to Grumble" has been our slogan, too. Relying on the Lord for spiritual feeding is vital to make it through transitional times. And our right attitude to the changing process is just as vital. Since the complaining spirit comes through that little member, our tongues, we will get through our deserts faster if we guard our mouths a bit more. If we did, we may not taste as much bitter water and may not get poisoned by as many snakes.

> But no man can tame the tongue. It is an unruly evil,
> full of deadly poison. Does a spring send forth fresh
> water and bitter from the same opening?
> —James 3:8, 11

When Is a Complaint Not a Complaint?

So what exactly are we talking about here? What is a complaint? If we see something wrong, are we not allowed to comment on it? What if yesterday's sermon really *did* leave you hungry? What if you feel you are truly not being fed in your desert place?

I was pretty sure I wasn't a terrible complainer. When I used to protest about something, it was surely the result of an appropriate desire to see wrong things put right. The situations justified my reaction; after all, I could produce biblical reasons for my opinions. But then I asked the Lord to teach me about what *He* considered a complaint.

He gave me an attitude test, asking me if I ran the issues past His desk before any other departments. I soon recognized that every now and then I did indeed head for people before I approached Him. All too often my complaints were when I was not submitting my weary emotions to the Lord for a check before subjecting others to their negative effects! I also realized that when I did go to the Lord first, He diffused the situations for me, often by telling me to pray more about it and trust Him for a solution which He Himself would provide—and did!

GRUMBLE VERSUS HUMBLE

The Lord loves His kids; He wants us to talk things through with Him, and He would prefer we did, even if we happen to be angry, mad, hurt or hungry. If we take the other route, however, and grumble before we humble ourselves before Him, then the complaints snowball, growing and spreading their infection into other hearts.

Complaints are so often connected to provision, whether it is of food or otherwise. Can God provide for us? Is He sufficiently able to meet our physical and spiritual needs? A complaint is dressed in the clothes of doubt, lack of faith and disbelief and is really pride in disguise. Why pride? Because we think we know better than the Lord what our needs are and when and how He should provide. The Lord's ability to provide has probably held many more people back from fulfilling their destiny than we could imagine.

Pride is also seen when we complain about what other people dish up to us.

> Do not complain [sigh, groan], brethren, against one
> another, that you yourselves may not be judged.
> —JAMES 5:9

For you were called to freedom, brethren; only do not turn your freedom into an opportunity for the flesh, but through love serve one another.
—JAMES 5:13, NASB

But if we take on the role of a servant, we have no right to protest. Jesus humbled Himself, released His rights and became a servant—without complaint. Humility and considering one another more highly will go a long way to ridding our lives of a complaining spirit.

ROASTED DESERT QUAIL

Partridges, quails, food complaints: growing up in the desert, Hoglah would have seen and heard them all. Imagine the excitement when the first birds flew by! I can just hear her father, "Wow! What a wonderful God to provide us with so many fat, delicious birds after so long without something appetizing!"

Then, when the ground could no longer be seen for the fall of foul, Zelophehad's excitement might have waned slightly. "OK, Lord, I get the message. Can you stop the birds now? I can't move without stepping on them, and there's so much bird mess on my tent. My kids can't sleep for the noise, and I think I might be—aaaahatishoo!—allergic to feathers!"

ANGEL CAKE

Of course, quail was never the food the Lord intended for His people in the desert; He wanted them to eat the food of the angels and be satisfied with that.

He rained down manna for the people to eat, he gave them the grain of heaven. Men ate the bread of angels.
—PSALM 78:23–25

This was the original Angel Cake, the angels' bread, our Manna from Heaven. Quail may be fat and appealing, but this manna, representing Jesus, is the *real* meat:

> And Jesus said to them, "I am the bread of life. He
> who comes to Me shall never hunger, and he who
> believes in Me shall never thirst."
> —JOHN 6:35

Manna looked like coriander, had a pearly sheen and tasted similar to wafers made from honey. (See Exodus 16:20.) The word *manna* means "What's that?" because at first the people did not recognize it was from God.

It's that provision issue again! We sometimes miss seeing what the Lord is offering us because we are looking for the wrong things or we look in the wrong place. And then, when the Lord's provision arrives, we can voice those same puzzled words, "What is this Lord? This isn't what I asked for!"

But, however and whenever the Lord chooses to provide for our physical needs, we all share a wonderful feast in Jesus, the Bread of Life. And He feeds our spirits primarily through His Word.

The recipe for survival in the desert and good spiritual health is in reading His Word daily. And, just as manna required some processing, we must sift the Word through our minds, grind it into our emotions and beat back the enemy with it. If we do this, the heat of the desert days will serve as an excellent oven!

THE PARTRIDGE AND THE MOUNTAIN

"So, that was it, Hoglah," Zelophehad explained, "and you must always remember that whenever you have a need, the Lord will provide!" With that he finished the two days of quail story and tucked Hoglah into bed for the night.

"Papa, I'm so glad I'm not a quail!" Hoglah chirped, not quite ready for sleep. Zelophehad smiled and lifted his daughter's chin so their eyes could meet. "Oh no, my love, you

are much better than a quail! You are a partridge, my little mountain songbird." Hoglah smiled, contented in her father's affirmation. Her father stroked her hair and sang soft lullabies until she, like her sisters, eventually fell asleep.

A MOUNTAIN SONGBIRD

The partridge, unlike the quail, is a mountain bird found hidden in the crevices of the rocks.[2] Our inheritance as destiny-takers will always be found in the high places and in the right crevice, the Rock of Ages. Once in that safe place, like Moses, they catch glimpses of God's glory and reappear, transformed and empowered. (See Exodus 32:22.)

THE PARTRIDGE AND ITS MEAT

Partridge meat is rich and tasty, and so is the Lord's. His Word feeds, sustains and satisfies us through our desert days and long into our Promised Land. It keeps hope alive within us, points, refines, trains and encourages us along the way. Start on milk if you are not ready for meat yet, but make sure you get full cream milk, not skimmed: skimming through the Word does not make one fat. Once you have acquired a taste for milk, the solid food will soon follow. Destiny-takers have a passion for the best meat! It is ironic to talk about wanting to see our prophetic promises fulfilled if we rarely dig into the Word to dine on its richest meat. It takes study, organization, and good time management. Creating time for the meat of the Word is a matter of our will. Will we?

THE PARTRIDGE AND ITS SONG

The partridge is a bird with a distinctive, ringing cry. "Its ringing call-note, which in early morning echoes from cliff to cliff amidst the barrenness of the wilderness of Judea and the glens of the forest of Carmel...”[3]

A ringing call is a good description of the partridge song; another word for partridge in the Bible is "caller." This songbird calls people to wake up, like a flying town crier calling out, "Hear ye, hear ye, it's a new day!" Just as the partridge song awakens the dawn, so this prophetic cry announces and rouses God's people.

The people in Deborah's day went to the city gates and cried out for her to wake up and sing. There was a battle ahead, and Deborah's prophetic song, in addition to Barak's military might, was needed to bring down the enemy.

> Awake, Deborah, Awake!
> Awake, awake, sing a new song!
> Arise Barak and lead your captives away!
> —JUDGES 5:12

Deborah's song was important for breaking the oppression that the people had suffered for twenty years. The prophetic song also relieves barrenness and gives hope, lifting spirits and bringing breakthrough. It puts the wind of the Spirit under wings for flying and soaring over difficulties, obstacles and mountains. Over weakness, the song calls forth strength; over pain, healing; over rejection, acceptance.

David, the great expert in worship, knew this and sang out the truth of God's character when he was in a tough situation fleeing from Saul's murderous intentions:

> I will sing and give praise. Awake, my glory! Awake, lute and harp! I will awaken the dawn. I will praise You, O Lord, among the peoples; I will sing to You among the nations. For Your mercy reaches unto the heavens, and Your truth unto the clouds.
> —PSALM 57:7–10

RESONANT AND VIBRATING

The songs of Deborah and David demonstrate an important principle: the need to focus on God, who He is and what He has done. In Deborah's song we see the villagers by the wells were singing of God's "righteous acts" (Judges 5:11). In David's we hear of God's mercy and truth ("faithfulness" in some translations).

Hoglah's name reminds us to bring together meat and music—the meat of the Word with worship. Just as the cry of the partridge cuts through the morning air, so worship in song blended with the Word of God pierces the atmosphere like a sword.

When worship, intercession and the prophetic blend together with the Word, the combination is very powerful. Each on its own causes vibrations, but when flowing together, led by the Spirit, the vibrations intensify—they become resonant. Our intercession becomes more intense, our prophetic declarations more focused, our worship enriched.

This resonant worship touches the heart of God and brings Him great pleasure. And it changes us too. We are transformed so we can face situations with God's power. The vibrations from resonant worship change the spiritual atmosphere, causing the walls of our prisons to shake and collapse, releasing us (families, churches, cities and nations) into our purpose and destiny.

A resonant song is clear. It amplifies God's truth until we can hear it deep within our spirits, the right song for the right season. Now our voice range may not take us to the highest notes, but resonant worship will take us to new heights. And we may take someone else with us. We can sing our prayers over someone else, and if it is a resonant song, even if the voice is untrained and haltering, it will soothe their hearts.

Best of all, the Lord sings a resonant song over us!

HOGLAH

The LORD your God is with you, he is mighty to save,
he will take great delight in you, he will quiet you with
his love, he will rejoice over you with singing.
—ZEPHANIAH 3:17, NIV

A PARTRIDGE IN A PRAYER TREE

While we are called to "sing a new song" to the Lord, and
many of them will resonate with freshness and life, there are
some old songs that still send their vibrations down
through the centuries. I love the old Wesley songs for their
depth and understanding.

Bold I approach the eternal throne and claim the
crown through Christ my own![4]

I cannot sing this song without it stirring courage in my
heart to move on and take my inheritance. There are many
magnificent songs we can choose from, or we can simply
pick up our Bibles and begin to sing. I was born again into a
Scottish Presbyterian church, where we regularly sang
through Psalms and other portions of Scripture, so singing
through the Bible is not a strange idea to me.

Once I was relaxing, singing softly through Song of
Songs, and my eight-year-old son crept in beside me on the
sofa and joined in. We sang about doves' eyes and tender-
ness, about love and lilies, banners and brides. The words
did not rhyme, but that did not matter; we had rhythm and
melody as we explored ways to express what we were
reading. We are not talking great song writing stuff here but
simple hearts singing simple words. How delightful it was!

When we reached the end, Jared piped up, "Mum, can we
do Revelation now!" Dinner had to wait while we fed on the
Word and sang our way through the bits of Revelation we
understood. This time we sang about eyes of flaming fire,
angels with trumpets, scrolls and open doors. Much of my
Bible is highlighted and underlined so it was easy for even a
child to spot the key phrases and sing them out. The two

books, following the highlighted phrases, probably only took us about forty minutes to go through, but the songs we sang still resonate in my mind to this day.

If you are shy, don't let that stop you—go swing your singing sword and let heaven be your only audience. But if any kids are around you, grab them, snuggle up on a sofa and give it a try. You might find you have a little Partridge in a Prayer Tree right there at home!

SONGS OF THE NATIONS

The flavor of our song will depend in part on the environment we are in and our cultural roots. Scots are drawn to Celtic type reels and refrains and also to the Psalms; in all my travels I have never heard Psalms sung as frequently as in Scottish churches. The Chinese have haunting, often melancholic melodies that draw out the beauty of nature: blossoms, rivers and skies.

Each nation has its own redemptive song, seen especially in its indigenous people. Africans have a gift of rhythm, and the Filipinos are a particularly gifted musical people, blending Spanish and Asian influences in their songs. The instruments used, of course, are as varied as the music: the Africans have a way with drums, the Filipinos with guitars—and, some might argue, the Scots with bagpipes!

As an East-meets-West family, we have had some interesting musical moments. On our wedding day, a multicultural affair, Kai Seen and I sang a farewell song in Chinese during the traditional Scottish, *ceilidh*, (dance) part of the evening. Our home collection of music brings out our eastern connections. One Chinese CD we have blends sounds from nature with songs from the Mongolian Plains: rushing wind is followed by the thunder of galloping horses, then a high-pitched cry of a young rider ignites the air as the song takes off. It is Chinese, powerful and prophetic, the effect breathtaking. I would love to hear a Mongolian believer singing in worship with a heart's cry like that! Since we have also lived as a family in several other nations, some of their music has rubbed off on us.

Many might consider "hillsong" to be the Christian music voice of Australia, but Aboriginal Australians have their unique worship style. Once we sat around an evening campfire in Arnhemland, the Northern Territories, as guests of a Christian Aboriginal community. We experienced their quiet, gentle worship, faces partially concealed in the darkness above the firelight, but hearts very much aglow. One song, "Holy Spirit Kukim" ("cook him" referring to the fire of God falling), had such a strong anointing that people were falling under the power of God, their only carpet the red earth of the Outback. No one played the didgeridoo during our time there, but I was delighted to see young boys racing around blowing out music on old vacuum cleaner tubes! Many Aboriginal worship teams use the didgeridoo, an instrument with a pulse that pierces the air and stirs deep within the spirit of Australian people.

Whatever our culture, there is a special sound and song for resonant worship in that nation. Imagine what the sounds of heaven will be like when we bring them together with the songs of the angels!

Zelophehad's third daughter lived up to the meaning of her name. I imagine she had a lovely voice, but if not, she certainly had a good refrain. Hoglah's call for inheritance woke people up to God's concern for women in need and resonated down through the generations so that the vibrations are still being felt today.

Hoglah did not fall asleep quickly that night. She was enjoying her father's undivided attention while her sisters were asleep. Tonight he was all hers. Zelophehad had worked his way through all the usual favorites and was now making up the songs as he went along. He sang a line and Hoglah, with an increasingly dreamy voice, repeated it after him.

"One day soon...I will see my land...flowing with milk and honey." It was a song Hoglah never forgot, one that, in those early years of her life, instilled in her great courage. Zelophehad, kneeling beside his little one's bed, stroked her hair gently. She was drifting off to sleep now, and he gazed on her soft features with pleasure.

"How rich I am, O God," he whispered into the night, "You promised us a feast in the desert and what a lovely feast this one is!"

HOGLAH: FESTIVALS AND FEASTS

In addition to "partridge," Hoglah's name can also mean "feast" or "a holiday to her soul."[5] We see this more clearly when we spell her name *Choglah*. *Chog*, the first part of the name, means "feast" and "dancing with joy." It is a fitting name for a baby born in the desert because the people had been called initially into the desert by the Lord to celebrate a feast. Zelophehad went for a feast and ended up with a feast of girls. I can just see chubby little Choglah dancing and twirling around at one of the celebrations, enjoying the party!

The seven Jewish feasts link God's people back to their history as well as pointing forward to God's purposes and promises. They were a shadow of things to come and a type of Christ. (See Colossians 2:16–17; 1 Corinthians 10:1–6, 11). They set a pattern of heavenly things on earth and were a time of either getting hearts right before God or of celebration. The feasts gave the opportunity for all ages and races to gather and pass on the baton of faith. The feasts are there to point us to Jesus.[6] Studying the feasts is fascinating. We will only have a quick overview of them here to whet our appetites!

THE FEAST OF PASSOVER, *PESACH*

Passover points us back to the Israelites' last night in Egypt, when a lamb had to be sacrificed. On Passover, at three o'clock in the afternoon (the "ninth hour"), the lamb was sacrificed and the high priest said, "It is finished!" This feast points us forward to Jesus, the Great High Priest, who perfectly fulfilled Passover on the cross, right down to the timing of His death at three o'clock.

THE FEAST OF UNLEAVENED BREAD, *CHAG HAMATSOT*

This second feast starts on the day after the Passover sacrifice. It lasts one week, during which the people eat unleavened bread, *matzah. Chag HaMatsot* points us back to the sudden exit from Egypt, when the people had no time to add leaven to their bread before leaving. (See Exodus 12:13.) Leaven, symbolic of sin, had to be left behind so they could move on as God's people. It took a desert to purge enough leaven from Hebrew hearts to move them into their destiny. (See 1 Corinthians 5:7–8.)

Eating matzah for a whole week requires self-control to cope with the boredom of such bland food. The Jews today play humorously on the word, referring to it as *matzot,* meaning "bread of affliction." Matzah represents Christ's afflictions: it is striped, pierced and burned in such a way that it appears bruised. Does that sound familiar? (See Isaiah 53:5.) Matzah is well-oiled bread, representing the anointing oil and the Anointed One, Messiah. This feast points us forward to Jesus, the Bread of Life, born in the House of Bread (Bethlehem).

THE FEAST OF FIRSTFRUITS, *BIKKURIM*

The Feast of Firstfruits celebrates harvest and the giving of the choicest sheaf to the Lord. This feast pointed back to

God's provision for His people and calls them to honor Him in their giving. Several events took place on this particular day: Noah's Ark rested on Mount Ararat; the Red Sea was crossed; the first fruit of the land was eaten; Haman, a type of the anti-Christ, died; and Jesus was resurrected. This feast points forward to Christ as our firstfruit and to His resurrection. Today Jews celebrate the Feast of Firstfruits in prayer.

THE FEAST OF PENTECOST, *SHAVOUT*

Pentecost is one of the better-known feasts. It is also known as the First Trump. It pointed back to the giving of the law, fifty days after the crossing of the Red Sea. (See Exodus 32.) It points forward to the outpouring of the Holy Spirit in Acts 2.

When the law was given, 3,000 people died as a result of the golden calf episode. On the day the Spirit was given, 3,000 people came to new life. And the language changed. For years the people had lived by the language of the law, but now they were free to live by the language of the Spirit, expressed in the diverse tongues spoken. Both events involved fire.

Pentecost was not just a "happy-clappy" event; the poor and the stranger were cared for as the harvest was taken in. The Book of Ruth, which expresses these themes of care and provision, is read during Pentecost. Pentecost in Acts takes this theme of caring and sharing and presenting the good news to strangers.

THE FEAST OF TRUMPETS, *ROSH HASHANAH*

This feast is the Second Trump and is held on the first day of the Jewish civil calendar, in autumn. White clothes are worn, and the people repent for their sins as the trumpet blows. No one knows exactly when the trumpet will sound. The Feast of Trumpets pointed back to a call to worship and repentance, a time for inner, reverent reflection concerning our sins. This feast points forwards to the sounding of the trumpet in the last days, the return of Christ and the resurrection of the dead.

THE FEAST OF ATONEMENT, *YOM KIPPUR*

This feast celebrates the third and Final Trump. The time for inner reflection is now over, and the sins realized are now confessed and atoned for. The Final Trump pointed back to when the high priest entered the Holy of Holies, and a scapegoat bearing the sins of Israel was sent off to *Azazel* in the wilderness. (See Leviticus 16:10.) This is the most sacred day of the Jewish year, when Israel comes together in self-examination, repentance and worship. Atonement points to the finished work of the cross and to the last blast of the trumpet.

THE FEAST OF TABERNACLES, *SUKKOT*

Sukkot is a joyous occasion pointing back to the booths in the desert at Succoth, which symbolize God's protection. Jewish tradition includes the offering of seventy bullocks for the seventy nations of the world, showing the Lord's desire to protect all humanity. As the Feast of Lights, it points forward to Jesus, the Light of the World, to His birth as He tabernacled among men and to the heavenly tabernacle.

THE WEDDING FEAST

God wants His people to meet Him, even in deserts, for a feast. He wants His people to celebrate joyfully with one another in good times and in hard. Two Jewish feasts originated, not in the desert, but in times of national victory: the Festival of Lights (*Hanukkah*), a celebration of the rededication of the Temple and the Festival of Lots (*Purim*), connected to the story of Esther.

Jesus is the fulfillment of all the Jewish feasts, and as Christians we particularly celebrate His birth and resurrection at Christmas and Easter. Whether we still choose to celebrate the symbolically rich Jewish feasts is a matter of personal preference.

Hoglah reminds us to feast on the Word, to sing out our songs and to experience joy. When we are going through a difficult desert time, we must take some time out to feast on the Lord, enjoy our families and do something fun to lighten our spirits! Our God is a God of joy and celebration. He loves a good party. After all, as part of our inheritance from Him, He invites us to what will surely be one of the best of all time, the Wedding Feast of the Lamb! (See Revelation 19:9.)

Zelophehad's girls were soon all asleep, but their father continued singing softly over them the songs he had learned from Moses and Miriam in the early days of deliverance. The desert wind howled loudly outside, but even so, his wife could hear him. She joined in quietly, and together they feasted on the Lord's goodness, feeling safe and secure inside their tent. And three small girls slumbered sweetly on.

CHAPTER 7

Milcah

*Z*elophehad and his wife soon knew another child was on
the way. Having endured three desert pregnancies
already, Mrs. Zelo was well used to the hardships. Nonetheless,
Zelophehad did everything he could to make his wife feel like a
queen, even if her throne was one of rocks and her carpet one
of sand. Zelophehad affectionately called his wife "Your
Highness" and ran to fetch whatever it was she needed at that
moment—if it was at all possible. One day he did manna collection duty, normally a woman's work, and the next he was
trying to find the clearest water in the campsite because his
wife had a thing about "not drinking water with bits in it."

Mahlah joined in the family fun, decided she was a queen too
and scrounged some purple fabric from the tent next door to
wear as a fake robe. She recruited her little sisters in the game
giving them on good days the rank of princess, but more often
than not they were her royal servants. They cheerfully obliged

and toddled around after their sister's every command. Watching their girls play brought a melancholy joy to Zelophehad; his father's heart reveled in their fun, but deep inside he longed for the day when he could build a home and they could all settle down and enjoy it, even if it would never be a palace.

"You know, Zelophehad," said his wife one afternoon after the girls had played princesses all morning, "I think the real royal one is this baby inside me." She patted her belly. "It's as if he thinks he rules my body, look!" They both looked down to see her belly contort as the baby within decided to flip over and try another position.

From that day Zelophehad switched the title of Royal Majesty from his wife to their unborn child and the family joke developed a whole new angle. Of course, he said all the right things about "as long as the child is healthy," but things seemed different this time around, and it raised his hopes. First of all, the baby was far more energetic than the girls had ever been in the womb. And then his wife kept referring to the unborn as "he" or "him"; previously, their babies had been "it" until they knew for sure. Secretly, Zelophehad longed for a son and he knew many members of his family also held their breath for a boy.

But it was not to be. Zelophehad's wife pushed hard and a tiny girl's head crowned as she made her way into the world. Zelophehad gently took his fourth daughter from the midwife and held the tiny body close to his heart for a long time. His mind raced back to his firstborn and the trauma surrounding that birth but now all he could feel was an overwhelming sense of gratitude.

"Oh Lord," he closed his eyes and prayed, "thank You for this miracle. You do all things so well!" Yes, Zelophehad had desired a son, but his newborn immediately won his love. He rocked the sleeping baby in his arms and marveled at the delicacy of her tiny fingers. "We were right, this is a child born for royalty," he thought, smiling to himself.

So rather than expressing disappointment with another

girl, Zelophehad showed his pleasure by bestowing on her a mighty title. "Princess" (Sarah) would have been a pretty enough meaning, but Zelophehad, in naming her, went one step further and claimed for her the top royal badge—Milcah, meaning "queen."

History's Queens

I asked my son what things a queen might say. He must have been reading *Alice in Wonderland* because he responded, in his best Queen of Hearts voice, "O-O-Off with her head." Monarchs down the ages have balanced privilege and responsibility in quite different ways. History, from both textbooks and the Bible, records their successes and failures, leaving a trail of lessons for us to learn from.

African queens are particularly interesting. Take Cleopatra VII for instance. She was a smart and strategic young queen who at seventeen expanded her empire by gaining Mark Anthony and Julius Caesar as allies. Cleopatra's reign came to an end when she became disheartened and chose to die by pressing a poisonous snake against her heart.

Another African queen, Amina of Nigeria (1588–1589) learned military skills from her warriors and used them to expand her kingdom. She is known for constructing protective walls around her military camps. Queen Amina listened to her people, protected them and gave shelter when they were battle weary.[1] Queen Nandi of Zululand (1778–1826), the mother of Shaka Zulu, is remembered as a symbol of hard work and determination, while Queen Nehanda, (1896) the grandmother of Zimbabwe, is remembered more for her organizational skills.[2]

And of course, since I am a Scot, Scottish queens are of great interest to me. A memorable quote concerning Queen Mary I says, "Her mind may flap about like washing on the line, but touch her right to the throne and she'll stand as firm as a rock!"[3]

Flapping minds believe one day and doubt the next. They trust for a while then become overwhelmed with worry. Queen Mary, for all her royal foibles, reminds us to stand firmly on who we are in Christ—a royal priesthood of people. The other queens mentioned highlight important skills or strategy needed to rule well: organization, hard work, determination and concern for others. And of course, Cleopatra's sad demise reminds us of a serpent enemy who uses discouragement and other vices to destroy our lives.

FAIRY TALE QUEENS

Many of us had our first introduction to the words *king* and *queen,* not in textbooks, but in bedtime stories. Traditional children's tales from around the world tell how sweet princesses become queens, often after great trials at the hands of the wicked. Most Christians know they are called to rule and reign with Christ, but sadly many stay permanently as princes or princesses, holding only the promise of future rule but never experiencing it. So how does a princess become a queen? The route almost always includes deserts, trials or disappointments.

Think about the parallels to our faith journey in the story of Cinderella. She sat in the ashes resigned to her slavery. A messenger arrived and told her she had an invitation to the ball, and supernatural provision was available for her. She was given appropriate apparel, including designer-made shoes. Simple earthy produce and scurrying rodents became her vehicles to meet Prince Charming. Cinders thought she had blown things as the clock struck and her ashen state was exposed, but the enamored prince tracked her down. With a loving look, he proclaimed, "If the shoe fits, you are mine!" Cinders moved from the gutters of life into a life of love and royal privilege. The ugly sisters who had mocked, jeered and abused her were soon disgraced.

Snow White lived a stunted life in a home designed for small people instead of residing in a palace. She opened the door to a seemingly harmless old lady selling apples. Reminiscent of Eden, the fruit is poisoned and she falls into the sleep of death. The prince awakens his love with a kiss and takes her as his bride.

We see the same thing in Sleeping Beauty where the princess comes under a curse, pricked at the spindle of disobedience, and is sent into a deep sleep. A prince on a white horse breaks the curse with a kiss of love and sets Sleeping Beauty free.

Jesus has issued an invitation to the ball. Many hold their invitations in their hands but still sit in the ashes, stuck in various inner prisons, resigned to a life of slavery. They know they have royal blood but are unable to tap into their destiny. Ugly sisters of jealousy, control and fear intimidate them into thinking they will never get to the ball.

But His story tells us our Prince has come, exchanging our rags for stunning clothing and unveiling designer-made plans for our lives. The Rider of the White Horse, Prince of Peace, breaks the curse of sin and awakens His bride with a kiss.

THE KISS

The Lord wants to kiss us—and be kissed in return. Song of Solomon opens with the bride's desire for an intimate kiss.

> Let him kiss me with the kisses of his mouth—for your love is more delightful than wine.
> —SONG OF SONGS 1:2, NIV

This is a picture of a full-blown, extravagant love affair. Some may be shocked, but this is a "type," or word picture, of Christ's love for the church. The kiss happens in our spirits, not with our physical lips. It is pure, holy and passionate. The kiss is to awaken the bride. It takes a slumbering princess from her ash heap, or personal desert, and makes her a queen. Without this deep, intimate relationship she cannot rise into her call or rule, with Christ over the land of her destiny. So what exactly is this kiss, and how do we receive it?

The Solomon "kiss" is "a gentle touch on the lips" with a root meaning "to kindle, to burn and make a fire." Just as a physical kiss can lead to a physical yearning or burning, so a spiritual kiss can cause our hearts and spirits to be consumed and burn with passion for more of the Lord.

CLEOPAS IS KISSED

The story of the disciple Cleopas gives us more insight into burning hearts. (See Luke 24:18.) Set between the resurrection and the ascension, this time was painful and unsettling for Cleopas. If ever there was a desert time for him, this was it. Yes, some of the women had told him stories about Jesus being alive, that they had actually seen him, but it all seemed like nonsense to him. Confused and hurting, he and a friend went for a seven-mile walk to see if some fresh air and exercise would clear their heads.

Cleopas and his friend walked and, most likely, talked through their shattered hopes and dreams. All they had given up to follow Jesus seemed wasted now, and then there was the trauma of the past few days—the rumors, arrests, the horror of the crucifixion and the ensuing grief. When they set out that morning, they did not know this walk would change the direction of their lives forever. So what happened? Jesus, unrecognized, slipped alongside them, listened to where they were hurting and then kissed them better with His words.

Just as the first kiss on a wound may well cause a person to wince in pain, Jesus' first deposit into their hearts, or "kiss," could well have been painful. He told them they were "foolish ones, and slow of heart" (Luke 24:25, NKJV).

How would you feel if, just after hearing a close friend had died, a complete stranger announced you were foolish to be sad? However, Jesus was not being unkind, but was hitting on their root issue. Their perceptions about their situation were wrong. They were paying more attention to their present circumstances than to the mounds of prophetic promises they had been given. Their hearts were not beating in time to the new rhythm of the resurrection. So, starting at the beginning, as He walked with them, Jesus rebuilt their understanding. With each word, their inner hearts began to tick faster until the master Pacemaker reset them to a new pace of faith:

> And they said to one another, "Did not our heart burn within us while He talked with us on the road, and while He opened the Scriptures to us?"
> —LUKE 24:32, NKJV

When a person awakens, he opens his eyes. Like the princesses in the children's stories, Cleopas and his companion were awakened to their royal destinies. But it was the eyes of their hearts that were gradually opening. The complete opening came later, over supper, when Jesus broke bread with them. Now they saw who this man was. Now they understood for themselves what the women had been trying to tell them. Now their eyes could clearly see their new destinies. And the first part of that was a test of their faith—Jesus disappeared. But their hearts were not discouraged this time, and in the dark of evening Cleopas and his friend turned around and raced home. Where the walk towards Emmaus was one of depression, confusion and grief, the journey back to Jerusalem was with hearts ablaze with the gospel, their lives forever changed by the words of Jesus: His kiss of revelation.

Walking is a good way to get close to God, after all God Himself likes to walk (Lev. 26:12). But we do not have to walk to Emmaus to find the Lord, although taking a stroll may help us to clear our heads. He promises us He will never leave us or forsake us. He is always beside us, speaking to us—if we will listen.

Walking through desert times can make us hard of hearing. Our hearts may be confused, hurting and puzzled over prophetic promises that seem to come to nothing. The outward circumstances yell to us we have heard God wrong. Hopes and dreams inside us have died. Every now and then someone comes along and tells us God is very much alive and working, but it doesn't seem to fit what we are seeing and experiencing. "Maybe," we wonder, "we should not have followed Jesus with such a passion; maybe we should have built up a life for ourselves instead of throwing it away on something that seems unobtainable." And then in those rock-bottom moments, the Lord comes alongside us and addresses our root issues. We may have to face some hard truths about the pace of our hearts, but the gentle kiss of awakening will do its work and ignite an excited response of love from us.

OUR KISS TO THE LORD

How do we respond to this resurrected Jesus and our awakened condition? We respond to the Lord's kiss by kissing Him in return. Our kiss is one element of worship.

> God is Spirit and those who *worship* Him must worship in spirit and truth.
> —JOHN 4:24, NKJV, EMPHASIS ADDED

The word *worship* here is *proskuneo*, generally meaning "to fall down prostrate, kneel or pay homage." One source, Strong, arguably, renders it "to kiss, as in a dog licking the back of a master's hand." My family owns two large poodles, but I do not really enjoy it when they start licking me! I know, however, they are demonstrating their faithfulness and showing how much they enjoy my affection. Worship, in some ways, is like a kiss to the Lord, done, of course, more reverently! It awakens us to His greatness, love and power, and fanning the flames of faith, it makes our hearts burn. The more we worship, the more we burn. Worship usually exercises both our lip and heart muscles, working together to give a beautiful, pure kiss to the Lord. Working lips without hearts is simply lip service—an empty kiss.

If all this has not inspired us to walk with God, read His word and worship, then there is more. The word *kiss* also means "to be equipped or armed." When the Lord kisses us, He does more than stick a Band-Aid on our wounds; His kiss equips us with clothing, our armor for the battle. See how many of the words in the following verse also appear in the armor chapter, Ephesians 6:

> Love and faithfulness meet together; righteousness and peace kiss each other. Faithfulness springs forth from the earth, and righteousness looks down from heaven.
>
> —PSALM 85, NIV

There is a divine exchange that takes place when we raise our lips to heaven.

Heaven kisses us with righteousness, which in turn brings us peace. We cannot do anything to get righteousness for ourselves; it is an act of divine love bringing peace between God and man. Heaven kissed earth on the cross, and that kiss arms us with a breastplate of righteousness over our hearts and shoes of peace, perfectly fit for a royal princess to go into the world sharing the good news.

Faithfulness and love also meet in a kiss. Faith on our lips meets with God's expressions of love. It works the other way around, too. Our expressions of love for God are met by His faithfulness to us. Every time we express to God our faith and love, sparks fly, igniting both our own hearts and the heart of God. And always it is God who has made the first move in this extravagant love affair.

We love, because He first loved us.
—1 JOHN 4:19, NASB

WAKING UP

So how do we know when we are asleep spiritually? We don't know until we wake up saying, "I must have dropped off!" Having said that, there are some things we can do to wake ourselves up. Call these things a "heavenly alarm clock." Firstly, we can position ourselves in the light.

Most mornings I am wakened by God's good sunlight shining on my face. Most of the time it wakens me just at the right time, but I occasionally resist its call and resort to unattractive airline eye masks. They work every time. Once the light is gone, I can easily go back to the "Land of Nod."

> Then Cain went out from the presence of the LORD and dwelt in the land of Nod on the east of Eden.
> —GENESIS 4:16, NKJV

This of course is a different Land of Nod. *Nod* here means "wandering like an aimless fugitive." When Cain murdered his brother and left the Lord's presence, his life became directionless. He was living in the dark instead of the light of the Lord, and it got him nowhere. Those who are sleeping spiritually are also aimless, unproductive and lacking strength.

Another way we awaken ourselves is to place ourselves around those with a prophetic anointing. Isaiah, Jeremiah and the prophets were Israel's wake-up call.

> Awake, awake O Zion, clothe yourself with strength. Put on your garments of splendor…Shake off the dust; rise up, sit enthroned, O Jerusalem.
> —ISAIAH 52:1–2, NIV

Isaiah was giving Israel not only a wake-up call, but morning exercises:

Rise up.
Shake off yesterday's troubles.
Throw away dusty rags.
Put on garments of splendor.
Sit down in heavenly places.

Wake-up calls come from the Lord directly, through a person with a timely word or through reading the Bible ourselves. These alarm clocks rouse sleepy believers to get up and enjoy a new day, dressed in royal style.

Queens are often figureheads of beauty and style, but these may lie only skin deep. Good or bad, whatever is in there will eventually be seen in the relationships with those around, particularly in our homes and marriages. The Bible has many accounts of royal marriages—some wicked liaisons, some anointed and others in between.

QUEEN JEZEBEL AND KING AHAB

There was nothing hidden about the wickedness and idolatry of Queen Jezebel and King Ahab. Jezebel "stirred" her husband up the wrong way with her cultic beliefs. She stirred the Lord's wrath even more by entertaining eight hundred fifty false prophets.

Ahab eventually died, his son and grandson were assassinated and Jezebel, now Queen Mother, ran for her life. She was chased by Jehu, trampled by chariots and eaten by dogs, her carcass becoming "dung in the face of the field."

Ahab and Jezebel are examples to us of how *not* to rule, under the rule of spirits of idolatry, manipulation and control. In fact, this spirit of Jezebel is so prevalent and strong it is mentioned in Revelation as a warning against self-appointed prophets who used their position to draw people into immorality. (See 1 Kings 16, 18, 21–22; Revelation 2:20–22.)

QUEEN ATHALIAH AND KING JEHORAM

Athaliah, the daughter of Jezebel and Ahab, was not much better. She and her husband King Jehoram of Judah both followed Baal and murdered family members. Her name means "afflicted of the Lord" and his, "God is exalted." God was not exalted—in either of them—but affliction certainly hit home. Jehoram, after killing his brothers, was afflicted with bowel problems and died. Athaliah took the reign, murdering almost all her family, but reaped her dues in the end. (See 2 Kings 11.)

Self-exaltation, inspired by idolatry, was one of Athaliah's biggest stumbling blocks. Ruling and reigning with Christ is never about exalting ourselves, but about making sure that "God is exalted." How Athaliah could have turned the tables in her nation, if she had taken to heart her husband's name instead of her own!

KING HEROD AND QUEEN HERODIAS

The New Testament tells us of at least one wicked royal family. Princess Salome, the daughter of King Herod and Queen Herodias, was from an incestuous family. She had a birthday party that would go down in history. Her father asked her to dance, and she gave a stunning performance. Pleased, Herod asked what favor she wanted in return, "ask and you will receive...even half my kingdom." Queen Herodias, angered by John the Baptist's prophetic honesty, seized the moment and hissed to her daughter a sinister instruction. Herod, more concerned about saving face than saving John's head, granted her request.

"Saving face" is fine when we are aiming to protect someone else, but when we are trying to make ourselves look good, it is pride. On the other hand, humility, a mark of God's royal people, understands we are who we are only by the "saving grace" of God.

MILCAH

PRINCESS JEHOSHEBA AND HIGH PRIEST JEHOIADA

There was little grace in Jehoram's depraved family, but there was some. His daughter, Princess Jehosheba was raised in his realm of wickedness, surrounded by it on almost every side. But she was a wise princess; she married a high priest, the only Jewish princess who did, and went on to save the life of her nephew, Athaliah and Jehoram's only remaining seed, their grandson Joash. Jehosheba hid the baby for six years until he could be anointed king, thus preserving the royal seed. Here was a princess who never wore a queen's outer garments but displayed queenly character. The godly influence that this princess-aunt and her high priest husband poured into the young king made a significant impact on their society and on generations to come. Joash ruled well, doing "what was right," as did the next three generations of kings of Judah.

Doing the right thing is not always easy; it could have cost Jehosheba her life, but it will always pay off, especially as a good example for the little people around us. Good royalty lays a foundation of godliness and sets an excellent example for the generation to follow.

KING DAVID AND HIS "QUEENS"

King Saul was ruled by fear of being overthrown by someone with a greater anointing, David, whose conquests made Saul's seem puny by comparison. Saul tried to ensnare David by offering him his daughter in marriage but his plan did not work—David's love for the Lord, and Michal's love for David, only served to make Saul more afraid. Michal warned David to run for his life and was then married off to someone else. (See 1 Samuel 25.)

David soon found himself a new wife, who bore the same name as Saul's, Ahinoam. Then along came Abigail. Abigail was not born into a royal family, but she married Nabal, a rich man, who was harsh and evil—and whose name means "fool." Nabal foolishly insulted David by refusing him food, but Abigail, with diplomatic deft, stepped in with provisions for David's men. It must have been a busy day for the lady, loading up her donkeys with two hundred loaves of bread, some wine, sheep, grain and copious grapes and figs. Abigail fell before David saying:

> Please, let not my lord regard this scoundrel Nabal. For as his name is, so is he. Nabal is his name and folly is with him.
>
> —1 SAMUEL 25:25, NKJV

And David, no fool, in turn fell for Abigail—her intelligence, quick thinking and beauty, combined with a practical hand—winning his heart. Nabal, on the other hand, on hearing what happened in his absence, lost heart and died ten days later.

After Saul's death, David was anointed king and brought his two wives to Hebron. As he grew in power, he added in a few more wives, eventually gaining Michal back, who left her new husband wailing tears of grief. (See 2 Samuel 3:16.)

Perhaps Michal never really recovered from being wrenched from her second love. She arrived to find David no longer the same man—but one with many other loves and a new tendency to be undignified. And the more David loved the Lord, the more she despised him and remained barren.

SOLOMON'S 700 CLUB

Now if King David had several wives, his son, Solomon outdid him.

> And he had seven hundred wives, princesses, and three hundred concubines; and his wives turned away his heart.
>
> —1 KINGS 11:3, NKJV

For all his wisdom, Solomon slipped up with his wives.

There was no way he could keep track of what the idolatrous queens were up to, never mind all their children. It was this "700 club" that let him down, led him away from the Lord and eventually caused his kingdom to fall apart at the seams.

I doubt that anyone these days could match Solomon's matrimonial feats or desire for women, but many have other desires that captivate their hearts, turning them away from loving the Lord. God wants a royal people with their hearts set on Him—and then blessings will follow.

QUEEN ESTHER AND KING AHASUERUS

Esther, Queen of Persia, is probably the Bible's best-known queen and the most symbolic of our lives in Christ. Born *Hadassah* ("myrtle"), Esther was orphaned and then taken from her uncle's home as a candidate to replace the belligerent Queen Vashti. But Hadassah (Esther) did not resist; instead she submitted, and "myrtle" became the "star" (after the meaning of Esther) and then a queen.

Esther followed the purification ritual laid down for every young virgin before they could enter King Ahasuerus' presence. For twelve months, fragrant oils were rubbed into her skin. During this time, Esther's wise cousin, Mordecai, continued to visit the palace and check on her progress, making sure she remained connected to her God and her people. Still, in spite of her pliable heart, there was some selfishness that had to be rubbed off, and Mordecai, in fatherly fashion, challenged her about it.

> For if you remain completely silent at this time, relief and deliverance will arise for the Jews from another place, but you and your father's house will perish. And who knows whether you have come to the kingdom for such a time as this?
>
> —ESTHER 4:14, NKJV

"Myrtle" was already becoming a "star," winning the

favor of many, even before she stepped before the king. Myrtle trees, like the eucalyptus, are renowned for their high oil content, which is released when the leaves are crushed. The tea tree is a good example, its oil being used for scores of different purposes, including cleansing and healing. It can even be used as anti-freeze! Young "Myrtle" was cleansed and in good spiritual health—and no longer frozen to the needs of her people.

But meeting the king on behalf of her people took a final, special effort. Esther knew she could not take upon herself this task alone or she might perish, so she led a three-day citywide fast and prepared to challenge the law before the king—just as the daughters of Zelophehad had done. Having adorned herself inwardly, she then took upon her the outer garments and was ready—to perish if necessary.

> On the third day Esther put on her royal robes and stood in the inner court of the king's palace...when the king saw Esther...she obtained favor in his sight; and the king extended to Esther the golden scepter which was in his hand.
> —ESTHER 5:1–2, NASB

What moved the King to bid Esther approach and touch his scepter? Her inner beauty. Others in the harem were, like Esther, outwardly beautiful, but it was Esther's inner beauty that set her apart, winning her favor with those around her, including the king. It was this favor that positioned her to save her own people, and God's, from annihilation.

As God's people, we are chosen for "such a time as this" to come into the King's presence, enjoy His favor and present requests before Him that will bring change in our land. Yes, we have royal privileges from the beginning, but becoming a queen takes time. As with Queen Esther, there are intense preparation times where dead-self cells are scrubbed off, and the Holy Spirit's fragrant oils are rubbed into the pores of our flesh. We will face seasons where breakthrough will require prayer and fasting. And like Esther, as a royal people, we have magnificent robes to wear.

> The king's daughter is all glorious *within*; her clothing is interwoven with gold. She will be led to the King in embroidered work; the virgins, her companions who follow her, will be brought to Thee.
> —PSALM 45:13–14, NASB, EMPHASIS ADDED

Today these are only inner garments, but they are manifested outwardly in our behavior and attitudes. It's what is inside that matters. We come before the Lord wearing the embroidered work of the Holy Spirit in our lives. Robes of righteousness are worn alongside garments of humility and praise, with other individual mantles tailored for our call. And the anointing process perfumes us with the fragrance of the Holy Spirit, exuding "love, joy, peace, longsuffering, kindness, goodness, faithfulness, gentleness and self control" (Gal. 5:22).

The Bible tells us these robes are white, but there is a golden thread running through them. Gold speaks of the refining process that runs through the fabric of our lives, removing impurities until we glisten with His glory.

How do we receive the robes of righteousness? Without Christ, all we have is like filthy garments to Him. But God operates a free laundry service, washing us with the best stain remover in the world, the blood of Jesus.

> Now Joshua was standing before the angel, clothed with filthy garments. And the angel said…"Remove the filthy garments from him." And to him he said, "Behold, I have taken your iniquity away from you, and I will clothe you with rich apparel."
> —ZECHARIAH 3:3–4, RSV

> And he said to me, "These are the ones who come out of the great tribulation, and they have washed their robes and made them white in the blood of the Lamb."
> —REVELATION 7:14, NASB

The word *white* is used to describe the wedding dress and means "as white as pure light": it is bright, radiant and resplendent. It is so white it actually exudes light, sparkling as if made of a thousand billion stars. This glorious gown is made of the finest linen, with threads representing the righteous acts of the church.

> For the marriage of the Lamb has come, and His bride has made herself ready. And it was given to her to clothe herself in fine linen, bright and clean; for the fine linen is the righteous acts of the saints.
> —REVELATION 19:7–8, NASB

I was pondering this verse late one night, wondering if the wedding dress was all ready, waiting on some divine coat hanger in heaven for us to slip into—after all, isn't Jesus our righteousness? However, the verse does not say *His* righteous acts, it says *our* righteous acts. As I questioned the Lord about this, He gave me a picture to help me understand. In my imagination I was taken to heaven's weaving department where I saw an angel sitting at a large loom. God's righteousness was complete and all lined up as glorious shining threads on the loom. Another angel was watching the church on earth, and every time a believer did a righteous act, he shouted to the angel at the loom, "Another one." The loom was pushed up one more time, blending His righteousness, with all its resplendence, into our small acts.

So what is a righteous act? It boils down to faith. Abraham's faith was "reckoned to him as righteousness," and so is ours. (See Galatians 3:6.) Since faith without works is dead, a righteous act is faith expressed in action. Remember our faithfulness is a kiss of love to the Lord? Well, here, each kiss becomes a stitch in the wedding dress of the bride. After a few thousand years of believers trusting and lovingly kissing the Lord in faith, our wedding dress must surely be getting its finishing touches. Imagine in heaven, as the bride of Christ wears this glorious dress, we might say to each other, "Look! That stitch was when you trusted God in a tough situation as a teenager."

"Here is where you still had faith to stay on the mission field when you knew it may have cost you your life."

"Remember when you put your last dollar into the offering plate? It's that iridescent sequin sewn on there."

Our faith brings eternal consequences, or "con-sequins" seen in our wedding dress, a perfect and personal gown, worn by the bride of Christ on her special day.

It was Milcah's special day. She awoke moments before dawn. By family tradition, the birthday celebrant received a surprise, sometimes small and sometimes big, but always homemade and always laid at the foot of the parents' mat on the evening before the big day. The gifts would be painstakingly made when no young eyes were looking, adding to the fun an element of surprise. Zelophehad's presents were often simple toys he had carved from blocks of wood. Milcah's favorite was a whistle, given before she could manage a blow, for a few years a constant companion. Whistle blowing was a common pastime for the children in Manasseh's camp, and "Zelo whistles" were much in demand.

But for Milcah, her whistle now seemed like an infant toy and was losing its appeal. Today, at five, she felt that at last she would join the ranks of the "big girls," catching up on her three older sisters. She thought of the gifts they enjoyed: Mahlah and Noah were into clothes while Hoglah had a thing about tiny beads in bright colours. These things, crafted by Mrs. Zelo, were the gifts Milcah dreamed of because they would mark for her the passage to being bigger and older and more like her sisters.

But then she was the "baby girl" and always would be. And besides, mildly disappointed, she knew her gift was not going to be from her mother. She had seen her father, beavering away with his back to her over the past few days. "Away with you, child," he had said on a few occasions during the past week, "you will see soon enough!" Grinning, he had hidden the object under his cloak, enjoying the tease. So she knew there was no new dress, at least not this year. Still, birthdays were fun, and now that her day was here, she was as excited as ever.

Milcah quietly removed her covers, stood up and peered around the tent in the dim light to see if anyone else was awake. Her parents slept at the back of the tent and her sisters by the door. Milcah's long-established place was right in the corner and she loved it there because she could string up a curtain and make a miniature hideaway for herself. Looking at her sisters, she saw Hoglah, normally an early bird, strewn across Mahlah's legs, using them as a makeshift pillow. Noah had also wandered in the night, but then that was no surprise; she never ended up in the same place where she had begun her sleep. Now curled like a dormouse, her head was inside an upturned manna-collecting basket. Milcah giggled at the sight. Sleep was still clearly in the air with all of them, and, the giggling fit now subsided, the only sound heard was of rhythmic breathing. She coughed loudly, hoping someone would stir, but lying there motionless, eyes closed, everyone seemed to be still deep in sleep.

It was only a few steps to where her parents lay, and Milcah knew she wasn't supposed to be here—not on this day. But curiosity got the better of her and she was soon at the foot of their mat, moving her hands along beneath it. It was not long before she felt a long, thin rectangle wrapped in soft old palm leaves. Milcah, ignoring rising guilt, tiptoed out into the dawn, sat down on the woodcutting block and began to probe the parcel. She had barely sat down when a deep familiar voice, coming from inside the tent, startled her.

"Up so early, my daughter?" She raced back into the tent, her gift clutched to her chest, stepping on arms and legs and hands and feet as she went, and collapsed onto her father's mat, breathless with anticipation.

"Please, can I open it now, Papa? Please?" Before he could answer, she had torn off the simple wrapping. Someone groaned, "Mil-caa-ah! That hurt!" Rubbing offended arms and legs, the older girls dragged themselves over for a closer look.

The object their sister held bore a skillful engraving—"Milcah."

She gasped, then hugged her father, then her mother, then each of her sisters in turn.

"It's beautiful, Papa!" Excitedly, she undid her plaited hair, the locks falling loosely over her shoulders, and using her new gift, she began to comb.

Zelophehad winked at his wife, seeing their daughter was already delighted. His little girl was growing up, and desert or not, girls wanted to look beautiful.

"There's more, Milcah," he declared, reaching behind him to retrieve a woven headband, decorated with silken flowers, secretly made by his wife.

"Mama, you knew!" Milcah could only gaze at it in amazement.

Floral headbands were the latest teenage girl craze, and although Milcah had a few years to go before reaching those years, here she was with one of her own. She felt so grown up, so loved and so beautiful that she thought her heart would burst with joy. Leaning over, Zelophehad placed the crown on Milcah's head and, accompanied by his family's claps and cheers, announced, "There. A queen needs a crown!"

CROWNS AND GARLANDS OF GRACE

A queen needs a crown. It is a symbol of royal position, victory and sometimes reward. Crowns are usually extremely expensive items. David's crown weighed in at a hefty seventy-five pounds (thirty-four kilos). That is roughly the weight of a ten-year-old child—imagine having one of those on your head. Some crowns are simple golden bands while others are ornately formed and bedecked with exquisite, sparkling gems.

The Bible talks much about the crowns we will receive. The basic crown, our crown of *righteousness*, is given to all who love Christ and long for His appearance, but there are different facets and jewels for us to add. (See 1 Timothy 4:8.) We all receive a crown when we become children of God, but our responses in life determine how much it will sparkle. And the desert is a good place to find wonderful gemstones. Gems, hidden where few can see them, are formed under extreme pressure; it is only when they have been extracted from the ground, shaped, cut and polished, that they display their true value.

When the Lord made man he intended for him to be crowned with glory and honor.

> You made him and crowned him with glory and honor.
> —PSALM 8:5, NIV

> And when the Chief Shepherd appears, you will receive the crown of glory that will never fade away.
> —1 PETER 5:4, NIV

Peter is writing to Christian leaders, reminding them that an *unfading* crown of glory is better than wearing a fleeting crown of superiority by lording it over others. This unfading crown is for those who lead others by example in an attitude of humility.

The crown is adorned with *wisdom, grace* and *splendor.* These are not grown overnight—even Jesus had to learn to be wise, increasing in "wisdom and stature" as a child. The gray haired amongst us will be pleased to know that gray hair is a crown attained through living a righteous life. (See Proverbs 16:31.) Thankfully for those who choose to hide gray hair, it is not the color of your locks that is important, but choosing to live wisely.

> Get wisdom…though it cost all you have, get understanding. Esteem her and she will exalt you; embrace her and she will honor you. She will set a garland of grace on your head and present you with a crown of splendor.
> —PROVERBS 4:5–9, NIV

Joy is added to our crown through the people we know and love; whether they are our wives, grandchildren or spiritual progeny we have led to Christ (Prov. 12:4; 17:6). Addressing the issue of squabbles in the church, Paul reminds his brothers they are his crowning joy. And crowns should not have their luster tarnished by bitter talk, but instead be garlands of grace sparkling with jewels of *loving kindness* and *tender mercy*. (See Psalm 103:1–6; Philemon 4:1–2; 1 Thessalonians 2:18–20.)

> The Lord their God will save them on that day as the flock of his people. They will sparkle in his land like jewels in a crown.
> —Zechariah 9:16, NIV

Let's be like English Beefeaters, protectors of the crown jewels in the Tower of London, guarding and adding sparkles of love, kindness and mercy to others' crowns. And if necessary by laying down our lives for one another and for the gospel, we will receive the crown of life, the martyr's crown.

> Be faithful until death, and I will give you the crown of life.
> —Revelation 2:10, NKJV

The desert is a training ground for those who want to run the race well enough to get a crown that will last forever. (See 1 Corinthians 9:25.) Bearing a crown sets us apart, in fact the Hebrew word for crown, *nezer*, means "set apart or consecrated." We are set apart to be holy, to love one another, to rule and reign over the flesh and to worship our God.

Queen Victoria knew what it was to wear a crown of authority, but speaking of Jesus she said, "I wish that He would come in my lifetime so that I could take my crown and lay it at His feet."[4]

Our crowns are designed for worship. Yes, they are a reward for us and will bring us pleasure, but the greatest pleasure lies in casting them down—a reverential act of deference to His higher power, authority and rule. (See Revelation 4:10–11.) Our ultimate crown, after all, is the Lord Himself. (See Isaiah 28:5.)

ROYAL REIGN, ROLE AND RULE

What is our domain? How do we rule and reign? Having the right clothing and a degree in monarch theology is one thing, but turning head knowledge into wisdom and understanding is what makes one truly begin to reign. The Lord is stirring his adolescent princes and princesses to want more; they are tired of game playing and of being defeated or apathetic.

This kingdom, however, is not like the world's reign and rule. We are called to be kings and queens in an upside-down kingdom with very different rules. Here are a few of them:

- Gain by losing.
- Get rich by giving.
- Live best by dying to your own desires.
- Rule by serving.
- Be promoted by bending low.
- Find strength in your weakness.
- If struck hard on the face, offer the other cheek, too.
- And the royal law: love your neighbor as yourself.

Does that sound like an easy way to rule? Isn't the royal lifestyle supposed to be one of luxury? Luxury and self-indulgence teach us little, but enduring difficulties trains us to reign.

> If we endure hardship, we will reign with him.
> —2 TIMOTHY 2:12, NLT

Two sisters, possibly twins, tucked away at the end of Romans, exchanged a life of ease for hard kingdom work.

MILCAH

> Greet Tryphena and Tryphosa, those women who
> work hard in the Lord.
> —ROMANS 16:12, NIV

Paul makes it clear that Tryphena and Tryphosa were
hard workers, but what is not obvious is the significance of
their names, translated "dainty and delicate" or "luxurious
and luxuriant." These names probably indicate Tryphena
and Tryphosa came from a life of ease and luxury. *Luxury*
means to "break up the mind and body by indulgence, a
softness caused by lavish living."

Misses Dainty and Delicate Luxury had to roll up their
sleeves because *work hard* means "to grow exhausted with
intense bodily labor or burdens." It is wearisome effort
linked to toil and trouble, rather like digging in dirty
ditches. Tryphena and Tryphosa toiled for the Lord, rather
than accepting an indulgent lifestyle.

Our daughter Kirstine took a year off between school
and university to do a Discipleship Training School (DTS)
with Youth With A Mission. She is a gentle girl, and when
she told us part of her outreach was working in a Thai
orphanage, we thought she had chosen well, imagining her
hugging babies and changing diapers. Instead, her days were
spent outdoors in the heat and humidity, digging a road.

Christian ministry requires exertion. It would be easier to
settle for a life of luxury, pandering to our own needs rather
than to those of the sick, the lost or the lonely. Once self-
indulgence is dug out, principally by hard work, our lives
become ditches and channels for streams of living water.
The desert is a good place for digging out self-indulgence.

> Opportunities are usually disguised as hard work, so
> most people don't recognize them.
> —ANN LANDERS, COLUMNIST (1918–2002)

We are not spared troubles or trials. In fact it is through
trials that we learn to reign well. Endurance tests our faithfulness and teaches us how to stand firm and solid until the

task at hand is done. Sir Francis Drake said, "There must be a beginning of any great matter, but the continuing unto the end until it be thoroughly finished yields the true glory."[5]

Hardship is a character factory producing "training for reigning," special running shoes to last the distance. It is not the sort of reigning we normally associate with royal rule on earth: full of power, pomp and ceremony.

> But man in his pomp will not endure; He is like the beasts that perish.
>
> —PSALM 49:12, NASB

God's kingdom has no place for pomp and pride. Pomp works contrary to endurance by making us soft and full of flesh. It's time to stomp out the pomp so we can last the distance and be good ambassadors for the King of kings. Any desire to be noticed or recognized reveals a heart of self-promotion. The only title we should desire, even as kings and queens in the kingdom, is "servant."

Desert life was no picnic for Milcah and her generation. They knew about endurance. They also knew little luxury. Privacy was well nigh impossible; the desert floor was hard and unyielding. This little queen grew up collecting manna, fetching water and carrying wood from far away, sweeping out endless dust from inside her tent, and walking miles in the hot sun. The character carved into her life in those tough early days later enabled her to reach for her destiny.

Milcah stole hearts at every stage of her life. As a baby, everyone wanted to hold her and hug her, and she cheerfully obliged. As a toddler she had poise marking her as a child with a special destiny. And with each stage of childhood, grace and dignity seemed to grow.

Now another milestone had been reached. As the sun went down on yet another birthday, its rays danced on her well-groomed hair, making it glow like gold. Milcah, lost in thought, watched the sun disappear, unaware of her father's gaze.

"If Hoglah is a partridge," he pondered, "then this one is surely a swan." He watched her for a few moments, wondering what her future would hold.

"Come my birthday queen, sit with me." Zelophehad patted the stool beside him, and together they sat, stately and mostly silent, watching the sun slip beneath the horizon.

CHAPTER 8

Tirzah

*Z*elophehad wondered if the strain of rearing four young girls was getting to his beloved. The conditions were pretty cramped in their tent, and he considered trading with someone who had a bigger one. His wife, however, declared she smelt honey in the air, and they wouldn't need another tent— the Promised Land was just around the corner. She didn't tell him she felt another baby move within her, but after so many years, she didn't have to—Zelophehad knew.

The cravings soon started again, only this time Mrs. Zelo was hankering after something sweet. Zelophehad asked around, but no one had anything that could meet her need. As far as his wife was concerned, desert food was no longer satisfying. She had caught a whiff of the land of milk and honey, and she wanted it. "Now!" Anyone who came near her tent heard a lecture on the benefits of honey and how simple manna-based diets would only work if something sweet was added to them.

Once when he was wood collecting, Zelophehad was stopped by an elderly tribesman. "You are too soft with that woman." Zelophehad knew what was coming next. His wife had been telling the Pregnant Wives Club how a milk and honey paste was nature's best answer for stretch marks. The old man went on, "She's created a honey craze!" Zelophehad nodded in agreement and smiled as a picture of his wife covered in sticky honey flashed through his mind. Not that honey was easy to come by in the desert. Occasionally a dead carcass would become home to a swarm of bees, and, every now and then, someone would find the small nest of a rock bee, laden with honey. No, his wife had just been stringing the women along—she would have been the last person to get into a sticky mess in the desert. The joke, however, got out of hand; a few believed her, and a few others were pestering their husbands with their sudden fancy for honey.

"Women have to be kept in their place, Zelophehad, or they take too much. Stretch marks indeed!" With that the old man hobbled off, shaking his head and muttering. Zelophehad's smile faded slowly into a look of concern. The talk about women having "their place" triggered deep emotions within him about the coming baby. As he walked back to his tent, his mind churned. He was yearning to get out of this desert, to build a home and settle down to some kind of a normal life. He dreamed of growing old in the Land of Promise and eventually passing on a rich inheritance to his family. But for that, for life to be normal, he needed a son. Without a boy, all this wandering would be in vain. He looked to the horizon. The sun had almost set, and the cloud was being gloriously transformed into the pillar of fire.

"God of burning fire!" A cry of frustration welled up within him. "If you can get water out of a rock and make manna fall from the sky, then where is my miracle?" Few still considered these as miraculous; they had become just a part of daily life, but for Zelophehad the wonder still remained. As the heat from the pillar of fire intensified and spread over the camp, so restlessness in the man's heart intensified as he wrestled with the expectations, not only from God, but also from himself and those around

him. He was tired of well-meaning people whispering "fifth time lucky" to him, and the spiritually inclined were no more helpful.

"If God can provide a lamb for Abraham, Zelophehad, then He will provide the son you need." Zelophehad felt if he heard the words "God will provide" one more time he would snap inside.

That night he dreamed that his wife had a multiple birth and produced seventy-five girls all in one day. He awoke in a sweat and sat up, expecting to hear the cries of multiple newborn babies. To his relief the soft sounds of peaceful sleeping were all that met his ears, but the dream was still vivid in his mind. Zelophehad arose quietly and went for a long walk beyond the outskirts of the camp where he wrestled with his thoughts until dawn. By the time the sun broke through, his mind and heart were clear. God was big enough to take a nation out of Egypt, and He was more than able to provide what the Zelo family needed.

Turning to walk home he stumbled on a low ridge of stone. He looked down and saw he had disturbed a rock bee's nest. The piece of rock he had broken off revealed a deep crevice the length of the ridge that was oozing with honey. Zelophehad grinned at the heavens and shouted at the top of his lungs, "God will provide!"

The day soon dawned when pain announced an imminent arrival. The excitement in the family was intense. Mahlah prayed her heart out. Noah ran backwards and forwards fetching water and giving progress reports to people gathered outside the tent. Hoglah sang songs of deliverance trying to ease her mother's pain. Milcah sat quietly in a corner, knowing that her long-held position of baby in the family was about to be removed.

The infant appeared, and Zelophehad gazed into bewildered little eyes, opening to the world for the first time.

"This sweet one," Zelophehad whispered proudly to his family, taking in the sight of his fifth daughter without so much as a flinch, "shall be called Tirzah." He gazed with affection at his wife who wept tears of relief that the fruit of her womb was acceptable.

TIRZAH

Zelophehad's choice of a name for Tirzah challenged the cultural hang-ups of the day. Tirzah *means "delighted with, pleased with, favored and object of affection." The root reveals an even greater depth to her name: "to satisfy a debt, to consent, to enjoy and to reconcile with self."*

What a list! Zelophehad was not only reconciled to the fact that he had another girl, he was delighted. She had his favor and had captured his heart with one glance from her bright little eyes. He gently scooped up his new treasure in strong hands, walked to the tent opening and carefully lifted her aloft for all to admire. "Meet Tirzah," he announced. "My highly acceptable, utterly delightful, most favorable, Tirzah!"

GOD-GLANCERS AND GOD-GAZERS

We are "Tirzahs" to the Lord. Over and over again in the Bible, we are told how acceptable we are to Him. We may think that we are human being number fifty zillion and one, but He is captivated by each one of us.

> You have stolen my heart, my sister, my bride; you have stolen my heart with one glance of your eyes.
> —SONG OF SONGS 4:9, NIV

All it takes to steal God's heart is one glance. A glance can communicate a thousand words. It might express pain, yearning, understanding or humor. The Lord sees our glances and reads them with expertise, compassion and love. We can glance from anywhere—the kitchen sink, the garden, the business meeting or the hospital, and our glances have an impact on the heart of God. Different translations of this verse draw out its richness:

> You have made my *heart beat faster* with a single *glance* of your eyes.
> —SONG OF SOLOMON 4:9, NASB, EMPHASIS ADDED

Thou hast *ravished* my heart.
—SONG OF SOLOMON 4:9, KJV, EMPHASIS ADDED

Just a glance and we ravish God's heart and make it beat faster. If this is what a glance does, imagine what happens with a good long gaze?

Another word for *gaze* is "behold." Hebrew scholars would know this word is represented by the letter *hey*, which is found not only at the end of Tirzah but in all five sisters' names. Playing on the English colloquialism, it's as if each name is exclaiming, "Hey, take a closer look here!" The letter *hey* is found twice in the name of Yahweh, a sign for us to behold and to behold again.

Behold is a good word in English too, when we tease it out: the Scripture says be still and know that He is God and *hold* on to what we have fixed our eyes upon. We hold on until what we have seen moves from our eyes to our hearts: a good gaze connects the eyes to the heart.

> For this people's heart has become calloused; they hardly hear with their ears, and they have closed their eyes. Otherwise they might see with their eyes, hear with their ears, understand with their hearts and turn, and I would heal them.
> —MATTHEW 13:15, NIV

Dull and calloused hearts prevent our eyes from seeing and our ears from hearing. Seeing eyes, hearing ears and understanding hearts are interrelated, and, when they are connected, there is no obstacle between us and the Lord, and we can receive healing from Him. No wonder the Lord so often instructs us to "Behold!" "Look!" and "Lift up your eyes!"

DELIGHTFUL

Tirzah's name means "delightful." Delight is a part of our Christian experience. When something delights us, it lifts our spirits; it makes us feel lighter within. True delight is hard to hide and harder to fake.

You may have heard of the water cycle, the cycle of precipitation and evaporation on the earth, but what about the delight cycle? It is a beautiful cycle of love. We delight in Him, and, in response to our prayers, He delights to grant us our hearts' desires.

> Delight yourself also in the LORD, and He shall give you the desires of your heart.
> —PSALM 37:4, NKJV

> The prayer of the upright is His delight.
> —PROVERBS 15:8, NKJV

Some may say, "But you do not know how pathetic my prayer life is."

"God cannot be delighted with me. My prayer life is a mess."

"The only prayer I seem to pray these days is 'God help me!'"

That may be how you feel, but persevere, knowing that the weakest and simplest prayer, from an 'upright' heart, delights the Lord's heart. He hears them all but sometimes sin blocks the communication channel hindering our prayers.

> Husbands, in the same way be considerate as you live with your wives, and treat them with respect as the weaker partner and as heirs with you of the gracious gift of life, so that nothing will hinder your prayers.
> —1 PETER 3:7, NIV

> Therefore be clear minded and self-controlled so that you can pray.
> —1 PETER 4:7, NIV

God calls us *Hephzibah*, "full of His delight," and invites us to a life in *Beulah*, the land of marriage to Him. (See Isaiah 62:4.)

What greater delight, or indeed destiny, could we have

than to be married to the Son of God? And knowing and experiencing His delight in us kindles our simple prayers and turns them into vibrant communication with God.

PLEASURE

Tirzah also means "pleasure" and, as we saw earlier, so does "Eden." God designed us for enjoyment from the very first days of creation, in the Garden of Eden, and has given us pleasure principles to live by.

One such principle is seen in our giving; when we give, we receive. Many seek to get their pleasure from material possessions, only to find the goods did not fill the desire for pleasure they had hoped for.

> Command those who are rich…[not] to put their hope in wealth, which is so uncertain, but to put their hope in God, who richly provides us with everything for our enjoyment. Command them to do good, to be rich in good deeds, and to be generous and willing to share.
> —1 TIMOTHY 6:17–18, NIV

Another pleasure principle is refusing to judge one another, lest we come into judgment ourselves. If everyone treated each other in this way, life would be a good deal more pleasurable for many.

Paul discussed this with the Romans, who were arguing over what food is clean or unclean. He asked them to stop passing judgments on one another, nor to put stumbling blocks or obstacles in their way. Instead they were to concentrate on the real issues in the kingdom of God: righteousness, peace and joy. If they served Christ in this way, they would bring pleasure to God and find their relationships with people much easier. (See Romans 14:13–18.)

> Behold, how good and how pleasant it is for brethren to dwell together in unity!
> —PSALM 133:1, NKJV

Pleasant words are like a honeycomb, sweetness to the
soul and health to the bones.
—Proverbs 16:24, NKJV

What a pleasant thing it would be for everyone if the
church was known for the "good life" where everyone was
generous in goods—and in attitude.

Relating to our brothers in a loving way is only one-half
of the pleasure coin. The other half, of course, lies in our
relationship to God.

The Pleasures of Praise

The Westminster Shorter Catechism's first question asks
about man's purpose in life: "What is the chief end of man?"
It answers, "to glorify God, and to enjoy Him forever."
Glorifying God is what our destiny is all about. And God
wants us to get real pleasure in doing it.

Praise the Lord. How good it is to sing praises to our
God, how pleasant and fitting to praise him!
—Psalm 147:1, NIV

In Your presence is fullness of joy; at Your right hand
are pleasures forevermore.
—Psalm 16:11, NKJV

If anyone knew the pleasures of praising God and
spending time in His presence, it was David. He knew that
his main "lot" in life was to be a worshiper and experience
the benefits that brought.

O Lord, You are the portion of my inheritance and my
cup; You maintain my lot. The lines have fallen to me
in pleasant places; yes, I have a good inheritance.
—Psalm 16:5–6, NKJV

The extent to which we worship, praise and enjoy the
Lord marks the boundaries of our destiny. Once those
stakes are in place, we can build our dream "home," and our

building contractor is "Wisdom and Sons": Wisdom, the builder; Understanding, the cementer; and Knowledge, the interior designer.

> Through *wisdom* a house is built, and by *understanding* it is established; by *knowledge* the rooms are filled with all precious and pleasant riches.
> —PROVERBS 24:3–4, NKJV, EMPHASIS ADDED

Zelophehad felt rich. He had none of the things so many men dream of and now, with the birth of another daughter, even Canaan's promises seemed out of reach. But with this new little one in his arms, he was as pleased as punch, and he knew his riches lay within his tent walls.

"Ah, Yahweh, I can see your hand on every one. You have made me a rich man indeed." And he rocked yet another of his babies off to sleep.

ACCEPTABLE

Tirzah can also be translated "acceptable." Deep inside every human being is a strong desire to be accepted. Once I was complaining to the Lord, wishing to belong to a certain group of people but feeling I did not fit in. I said, "Lord, I wish I didn't feel so different!" At my outburst, the Lord responded, using words I often sang to Him,

> There is none like you,
> No one else can touch my heart like you do,
> I could search for all eternity long,
> And find there is none like you!

I chortled and laughed on and off all day at the Lord's gentle and humorous way of pulling me out of self-pity. We are all one-off models, and the Lord accepts each of us just as we are, even if certain groups or individuals don't. It takes some time to let go of what other people think of us and be only moved by God's opinion, but what a feeling of peace comes when we finally know we are accepted by Him.

In Greek several words may be translated "acceptable." One is *dektos*, meaning "taking hold of by the hand, receiving friendship or hospitality and bringing one into one's family." This word, chosen by Septuagint translators, is used when the Lord says, "*Take* this cup" in the Last Supper.

When Jesus asks us to take His cup, He is inviting us into His family, showing us complete acceptance as His adopted children.

Desert times make us question if we are acceptable. The situations that drew us into the desert may have been afflictions, such as rejection by others. Or it may have been our own sin. Whatever it is, we must make sure guilt, true or false, or the enemy's whispered condemnation does not keep us there. We can confidently respond, "I am accepted and loved by God!"

FAVORED

Tirzah also means "favorable" or "favored." Favor is an intriguing concept because for many it raises questions about God's love for us. For instance, "Does God have favorites?" No, that's favoritism. *Favor* comes from blessing. And God desires to lavish his blessings on every individual, without favoritism.

The first time a blessing is mentioned is when God blessed Adam and Eve when they were first created. (See Genesis 1:28.) Living in a perfect world, everything was going smoothly for them, and they had a close relationship with one another and with the Lord. What more could there be in this sinless paradise? Well, there was more: the Lord gave them a special blessing, extra favor, and it brought multiplication, fruitfulness and a new ministry. It was not the only time when someone sinless was blessed—the new Adam, Jesus, also had to learn how to grow in favor with man and God before His ministry could be fruitful. (See Luke 2:52.)

Joseph knew a great deal about favor. His father's favor caused jealousies, which landed him in a pit. Potiphar's favor brought both blessing and trouble. Then the prison warden's favor opened prison doors for Joseph and set him in a prominent place, from where he in turn was able to dispense favor to others.

David was thrust into kingship, a position he never sought, because of the favor of God. Once king, he found himself in ever more sticky situations and continued to ask the Lord for favor. In battle, he knew that victory was a result of receiving it.

> They did not conquer the land with their swords; it was not their own strength that gave them victory. It was by your mighty power that they succeeded; it was because you favored them and smiled on them.
> —Psalm 44:3, NLT

David knew God had smiled on him, but he didn't let it go to his head. Twice he remarked, "But who am I?" knowing that without God, he was no more than a shepherd boy. (See I Samuel 18:18; 1 Chronicles 29:14.)

Mary found favor with God and was catapulted into His purposes for her destiny as the mother of Jesus. Favor here is *charis*, a Greek word also translated "blessing, grace, gift and credit." God loves everyone equally. He credits our account with gifts and blessings, but we must withdraw many of those blessings ourselves, by praying them into our lives. Those who spend more time praying, who have an ever-deepening relationship with the Lord, will experience more of His favor. That is what happened with the disciple whom Jesus loved, John. He spent time leaning on Jesus' breast; he liked to be close to Jesus. And he knew he was loved.

The early church saw how favor brought anointing in

their ministry and multiplication of the church. Still, they knew that God has no favorites, not even the Jews. His favor was accessible to all who lived righteously. (See Acts 10:34; Proverbs 14:9.) There is more. Favor protects us like a shield, strengthens us and brings us victories over the enemy.

> For it is You who blesses the righteous man, O LORD,
> You surround him with favor as with a shield.
> —PSALM 5:12, NASB

> O LORD, by Your favor You have made my mountain
> to stand strong; You hid Your face, I was dismayed.
> —PSALM 30:7, NASB

Favor often brings recognition and access to leaders of the land, as it did with Esther and, perhaps reminiscent of the daughters of Zelophehad, it led to laws being reversed and policies changed. (See Esther 2:17.)

SOLOMON'S TIRZAH

Tirzah is also the name of a city mentioned by Solomon.

> O my love, you are as beautiful as Tirzah, lovely as
> Jerusalem.
> —SONG OF SOLOMON 6:4, KJV

Now if my husband told me I looked like a city, I might throw a fit, thinking he meant I was dusty, polluted, overly busy and impersonal, but in Solomon's time these cities were places of refuge, growth, wealth and excitement. Tirzah, like Jerusalem, was a strong and beautiful city later becoming the capital of Israel, the northern kingdom. It was a city set on a hill, visible to all. (See Matthew 5:14.)

Solomon's beloved, likened to the city of Tirzah, was probably a young Shulamite shepherdess. We are not told her name, though Song of Songs recounts their journey of love calling them "Lover" and "Beloved." The Beloved,

Shula, as we will call her, had to face up to scars from her past and times when she could not find her lover. On two occasions she raced out into the dark streets at night searching for him—both times she met watchmen.

FIRST WATCHMEN ENCOUNTER

The watchmen's job was to ensure that the city was safe from danger and intruders. They were the city bouncers who kept out the "bad guys" and made sure those out at night were not up to any nonsense.

On Shula's first dark night, she raced into the streets, searching for her lover when the watchmen found her. If anyone could have given her some words of wisdom on where he might be, it surely would have been them.

> Have you seen the one my heart loves?
> —SONG OF SONGS 3:3, NIV

Whatever they responded, she had scarcely passed them when she found her lover. She might have written in her diary that night, "Next time I lose my lover, I know where to find him: right beside the watchmen."

A NEW SEASON

After this night is over, Shula, who represents both the church and each of us individually, enters into a new phase in her journey into love. Her young eyes have been opened to see more of her lover's glory and majesty, but along with that, she has a new insight into people.

On her first dark night of heart-wrenching searching, she had a new appreciation for the watchmen and was, in some way, helped by them. She was headed in the right direction and they let her pass without hindrance.

But now, in daylight, she saw more—sixty warriors, flanking the king's throne.

TIRZAH

Look! It is Solomon's carriage, escorted by sixty warriors…all of them wearing the sword, all experienced
in battle…prepared for the terrors of the night.
—SONG OF SOLOMON 3:7–8, NIV

But it is not just the midnight watch and the warring
people Shula notices, for the first time she sees the careful
work of others who have delicately inlaid her lover's throne
with pearl and gold. Its seat was upholstered with purple, its
interior lovingly inlaid by the daughters of Jerusalem.

Both pearl and gold are fashioned in the difficult desert
seasons of our lives. Pearl is produced by a healthy reaction
to an irritation, a particle of sand. Desert times blow into
our lives many little irritations, which produce pearls to
inlay on His throne if we allow them to. Golden inlay represents refining and fiery tests. Precious gems are inlaid too;
where the pearls result from minor irritations, gems come
from times of great pressure.

Desert seasons are times when everything presses in on
us, times when we feel that the Lord is far off. These are
often referred to as long dark nights of the soul, but those
who make it through come out with new insights into warfare, fresh throne room perspectives and a new
understanding of the Lord's majesty. And grateful for these
pearls of wisdom and golden nuggets of truth, we worship
God, inlaying His throne with our praises.

You…are enthroned upon the praises of Israel.
—PSALM 22:3, NASB

BLOWING IN THE WIND

Shula has a new fragrance, like a secret garden brimming
with exotic smells, and it pleases her lover. He sees that the
garden of her affections is watered by springs of living water
and flowing fountains. This is good. How he has longed to
get into the locked up areas of her heart! And she is ready to
allow him, no matter what winds may blow upon her life.

> Awake, north wind, and come, south wind! Blow on
> my garden, that its fragrance may spread abroad. Let
> my lover come into his garden...
> —SONG OF SONGS 4:16, NIV

South winds bring refreshing, healing and comfort, but
the north wind is not as pleasant. She knows that but calls
for them anyway, knowing both winds, both good times and
hard, draw her closer to her lover. The north wind blows
into the Shulamite's life a few nights later, bringing with it
testing and tribulation.

HIS HAND ON THE LATCH

Shula is in bed, and although her heart is awake invading
her dreams, her body is sound asleep. Suddenly, she is startled out of sleep by a loud knocking.

> Open to me, my sister, my darling, my dove, my flaw-
> less one.
> —SONG OF SONGS 5:2, NIV

Her lover is pounding at the door. She has dreamed of
this moment with keen expectation, but for some reason
now that it is here, Shula hesitates, her mind flooding with
irrational questions and thoughts.

> I have taken off my robe—must I put it on again? I
> have washed my feet—must I soil them again?
> —SONG OF SONGS 5:3, NIV

Yes, she is in love, but she was not expecting him tonight.
She is comfortable and warm, and the small amount of
effort required to get up, cross the room and open the door
is somehow too much for her. And goodness, a girl cannot
go back to bed with dirty feet. What if? Must I? Haven't I
done enough already?

With her voice she has been declaring her love, but her
actions betray her heart; perhaps she is not ready for this

new stage in intimacy after all.

Then she sees his hand and her heart begins to pound. (In Ancient Near Eastern villages, keys were stored beside the door on the inside, or, for some reason strange to us, outside. The keys were very large, up to a foot in length, and accessible from the outside of the door through a small hole—just big enough for a man's hand.)[1]

> My lover thrust his hand through the latch-opening.
> —SONG OF SONGS 5:4, NIV

Shula assumes her lover can reach the key, which will save her from getting her feet dirty. But, alarmingly, his hand withdraws, unable to reach the key to her special place of intimacy. She races to the door, her heart still pounding. Flinging it open, she is ready to throw herself into his arms…but he has left—he is gone. Shula's heart sinks. She had procrastinated too long.

SECOND NIGHT RUN

Racing into the night, with the north wind blowing strongly, Shula chases after him, searching frantically and calling his name. And then the watchmen find her. Relieved, Shula begins to ask them if they have seen her lover again. The words are barely uttered when she feels the first blow.

> They beat me, they bruised me; they took away my
> cloak, those watchmen of the walls!
> —SONG OF SONGS 5:7, NIV

No matter what she tries to yell out between punches she is not heard. The guards strip her cloak from her and pack her off, discarding her as they would a prostitute of the night. With every blow, questions raced through Shula's mind.

"Why? Don't you remember me from before? Don't you know my heart? I'm no prostitute! How can you think that about me? Are you not supposed to protect me?"

Those protectors of the city! Those watchmen of the walls! Confused, dazed and sore from the beating, Shula staggers to her friends' house and bangs on their door.

> I charge you—if you find my lover…tell him I am faint with love!
> —Song of Songs 5:8, NIV

Pressing On Alone

A woman to the core, she runs to her friends. "Well, if the keepers of my city won't help me then maybe my girlfriends will!" But her sleepy friends have nothing but a few questions for her:

"What's so special about him?"

"How is he any better than anyone else?"

"Is he worth all this pain and trouble?"

If there was a hint of sarcasm in their tone, Shula does not seem to notice it. Without hesitation she responds, "Oh yes, he is unmatched by any. His head, his eyes, cheeks and lips—his body and arms and legs. Everything about him is 'altogether lovely'!"

Many of us have shared in the Shulamite's journey. The Lord spoke to me in a powerful vision to teach me about this stage in my relationship with Him. It happened as I was worshipping alone, a thick presence of God in the room. In the vision I was standing outside a row of Scottish cottages, representing my home, culture and things familiar to me. Dressed in a bride's white gown, I was surrounded by many close friends from all over the world. They were dressed in bridesmaid's dresses, each wearing colors that suited them perfectly. They had been helping me to get ready for my wedding, and now the work was done. We were all waiting outside the house in eager anticipation, enjoying one another's friendship and the thrill of it all.

None of us heard Him come. Before we knew it, the Lord was right there, standing on the pathway. I knew if I followed Him on that path it would change me forever. We all looked up at Him, and I hesitated. I knew in that moment I could not take my friends with me, no matter how good they were and how much I loved them. This journey was for Jesus and me alone. I was torn inside as I heard Him call out, "Come away with me." I turned and looked back at my friends, and as I did, the Lord moved amongst them and caught my eyes with a gaze that said it all. "I didn't want to have to do this, but it will help you to get to the place your heart yearns for." He then went up to two of my friends and whispered to them. One of them promptly turned and walked away, and the other looked at me then turned her back on me. I was stunned and filled with pain. The Lord then looked at me and said, "Need I go on?"

Found at Last!

Shula goes on, searching, longing, desperate. Then, suddenly, it dawns on her, fresh insight interrupting her soul's dark night. She knows where he is. He is in the garden.

> I am my lover's and my lover is mine; he browses among the lilies.
> —Song of Songs 6:3, NIV

Of course, wasn't that where it all began, in a garden? Heartsick, still dirty and bruised, she races to the garden. She collapses in tears of joy and exhaustion as she sees him, standing there with lilies in his hands. He has been waiting a while, but he knew she would get there eventually. He smiles lovingly and says:

> You are as beautiful, my darling, as Tirzah!
> —Song of Solomon 6:4, NIV

His Tirzah was here at last—desirable, pleasing and acceptable. Looking down at her bruises, cuts and dirty clothing she responds, "How can you say that? I am so bruised, so weak and so dirty."

"I don't see dirt," her lover replies, "I just see your dove eyes and your beauty. Come away with me!"

Solomon's "Tirzah" did just that. And so can we—His Tirzahs.

Zelophehad looked at his little Tirzah in his arms. People were gathering around to catch a glimpse of her. The women were captivated immediately.

"Little dove's eyes, what a darling!"

"Precious little mite, Zelophehad, she is gorgeous!"

Milcah was by now desperate to hold her new sister, so Zelophehad sat her down securely and carefully placed the tiny bundle in his fourth daughter's outstretched arms. The men, who had been quiet until now, approached Zelophehad, shaking his hand and patting his back politely. Milcah's friends were beginning to gather, and eager arms were reaching out, begging to be allowed to hold the infant. Zelophehad stepped in and, taking the child back into his arms, suggested they all come back later. Milcah skipped off to play, realizing that her place in the family was secure, after all, and thinking, "Little babies are pretty boring."

With Milcah and her friends now out of earshot, the conversation changed to the lack of a son.

"Bit of a problem for you now, Zelophehad," said one.

"Another girl?" responded Zelophehad. "Not a problem—a delight."

"What about the land, Zelophehad? And your poor wife, how can she bear yet another child?"

Zelophehad smiled, and raising his eyes toward heaven he answered, "Jehovah Jireh, my Provider," and, with that, nestled his new daughter more tenderly into his arms and moved back into the tent.

CHAPTER 9

Character of a Daughter of Zelophehad

*Remember how the LORD your God led you
through the wilderness for forty years, humbling
you and testing you to prove your character.*
—DEUTERONOMY 8:2, NAS

Zelophehad breathed his last—then was gone. When their father made his final journey, to be buried outside the camp, five broken-hearted teenagers, clinging to each other, walked alongside. These painful steps were familiar ones; only a few months earlier, their mother had slipped away in her sleep. Now, with Zelophehad gone, the family tent seemed large and empty.

Friends helped as much as they could with practical matters. One old widow collected manna for the girls each morning, knowing they had wept their way through the night. Another kind soul left a pile of chopped wood by their tent, and someone else checked their tent pegs at dusk to make sure nothing blew away in the night. For the first few days, people came and went with hushed tones, but soon visitors were not as frequent, and life returned to a very different kind of normal.

Over the years, Zelophehad's generation died until now, with his departure, few older people were left, and many families were in grief. When Aaron, the high priest, died as well, it brought great corporate sadness. Still, six months after that, the camp felt like a new place, even for the five young women. Now on Moab's flat plains, the people seemed ready to scale a mountain. Expectation was in the air, and the Promised Land was beckoning the people forward. It was all anyone ever talked about these days apart from Census II.

CENSUS II

The Book of Numbers is so called because it contains a bunch of numbers. Using both facts and figures, it records the details of both censuses that Moses took. Known to the Jews as *Bamidbar*, "in the desert," this book details the first census, taken just two years into the desert season, and the second before the people entered their Promised Land.

> Then it came about after the plague, that the LORD spoke to Moses and to Eleazar the son of Aaron the priest, saying, take a census of all the congregation of the sons of Israel from twenty years old and upward, by their fathers' households, whoever is able to go out to war in Israel.
> —NUMBERS 26:1–2, NASB

The overall numbers had not changed much. Almost the same number that went into the desert came out. But the second census was different in one important aspect: it held the key to the up and coming land division. In this "numbers" game, each tribe was to inherit an amount of land according to the numbers within their tribal camp: the greater the numbers, the greater the portion of land for that tribe.

If people in the smaller tribes considered that unfair, they were careful not to express it. The last plague had dealt a strong blow to the complaining spirit. Besides that, it was obvious the tribal size was a reflection on their level of obedience to the Lord.

Another vital consideration was the question of *where* each tribe would settle, or "Who gets what?" The Lord did not want His people fighting over the answer to this—He would deal with it Himself, through a national lottery.

> Then the LORD said to Moses, "Divide the land among the tribes in proportion to their populations, as indicated by the census...Make sure you assign the land by lot, and define the inheritance of each ancestral tribe by means of the census listings.
> —NUMBERS 26:52, 55, NLT

We can only guess how this lottery was carried out. It seems that Moses drew lots determining the geographical position of each tribe, placing them northwest, southeast and so on within the new land. The extent of land each tribe received was a matter of how fruitful they had been, and this is where the census came in. Every head would be counted—that is, every male head of twenty years and over.

Moses listed their names by tribe, clan, then family, then each man, as he came forward representing his extended family, would bring an offering of half a shekel, the required ransom money, so that no plague would come upon them. (See Exodus 30:11–16.)

Men talked in huddles all over the place. The last census had been thirty-eight years previously, so for most of them, this was a new experience. Those in the larger camps talked openly about how much growth had taken place in their desert season. Judah with its lion emblem and loud triumphant praise had a lot to roar about; they had done well, going in with the biggest numbers and coming out just as strong.

Manasseh, the tribe to which Zelophehad had belonged,

entered the desert as the smallest tribe but had become the second largest. Even before the census took place, those good with figures had been able to calculate that their portion of land would be large, and everyone was ecstatic. Men gathered until late at night sharing their hopes and dreams and voicing wishes for where their lot might fall.

"It's all in the Lord's hands, Jair, my friend," declared Machir, a mighty warrior, "the land already has our name on it. But I expect we will have to go to war, my brother, before we can build our mansions."

The daughters heard that Manasseh's share would be one of the largest, but there was a dull ache in their hearts that Zelophehad's name could not be included in the land stakes.

"It was all he ever wanted, Milcah," Mahlah lamented quietly in their tent late one night. "A piece of land where he could settle his family in comfort and security."

"That's true," her sister replied softly, not wishing to arouse the others—in vain. Milcah relit the old family oil lamp, and the girls gathered around it, huddled in blankets, their faces lit up by the flickering flame.

"Remember what Papa said?" said Hoglah after some time, "'Don't forget the promise, girls. And dream big dreams.'"

Even as she repeated Zelophehad's words, tears welled up in young Tirzah's eyes, and she drew a small sigh. It didn't go unnoticed; the others all understood she missed Zelophehad more than anyone. Mahlah, who was like a mother to Tirzah now, drew her blanket up around her younger sister's shoulders and moved closer to her. Tirzah, being the youngest, had always found a spot on Zelophehad's lap when she was distressed, even when she was far too big to fit there comfortably.

"'Remember the stories of Abraham, Isaac and Jacob,'" quoted Noah, saying each name slowly, as Zelophehad always had, as if there was something holy about them.

Hoglah did not want yet another melancholy night and, always the witty one, broke into the hush, "Hey, don't forget *the women. What about Sarah and Rebecca?"*

The others smiled, relieved she had lightened the atmosphere. It was true, Zelophehad, in his storytelling, had always been careful to recount the exploits of the women as well as the men. Now, with sleep far from their minds, the sisters started retelling Zelophehad's favorites, one by one. They came to the story of Rachel and Leah, when they asked for their father Laban's inheritance, and something began to stir in their hearts—and in the tent. A strange, sweet breeze was wafting around them, causing Mahlah to stop her storytelling midsentence. The lamp flame flickered, dancing with the movement in the air. And then a heavy peace descended. They sat looking at each other, hardly daring to breathe.

No one was quite sure who thought of it first. It seemed the idea had dropped simultaneously into each of their hearts, yet, strangely, especially for Mahlah, it was as if it had been there all along, waiting to be expressed.

"'Dream big dreams,'" Hoglah whispered the words as if she hardly dared say them, and then again louder, "Dream big dreams!"

"Why not?" Mahlah said. "Why not, indeed? Why not?"

No one slept all that night, or the next. Their hearts were captivated with an idea so huge it made them race with excitement. Over the next few days it was the only topic of their conversation—when other ears were not around to hear. The men had been in their huddles; now these five women had one of their own. There were implications to consider.

"What about Miriam and Aaron? When they challenged the law, they nearly died for it."

"What about Korah? He did die!"

"Yes, but they were all thinking about their own rights. We're thinking about Papa's."

"But our father's name will be buried in the sand if we don't try."

And then, which one would approach Moses?

"I'm too young," Tirzah squealed.

"Don't look at me, I'm too emotional," Hoglah said.

"Well, I'd be scared out of my wits," Milcah offered, "but someone *needs* to do it. Count me in."

"Me too," declared Hoglah, Noah and Tirzah in almost complete unison.

"Yes. We must all go together," Mahlah affirmed at once, "or not at all." Heads nodded in agreement.

"We'd have to go near to the glory cloud." Hoglah had hesitation in her voice. "I've never been anywhere near the Levites' camp before."

"Let's go now," Noah declared, as impetuous as ever. "Get it over and done with."

"No," said Mahlah with authority. "It's dangerous enough at any time approaching the tent. To go at the wrong time could cost us our lives. Remember what our father taught us about patience and timing? We must wait for the right time."

So they did, until one morning when they all knew the wait was over. Today was Manasseh's day to line up for the census. The leaders of each family had already taken the record of their own numbers, and from sunrise they were heading towards the tent of meeting to present their finest men before Moses. This was Zelophehad's daughters' opportunity. They woke before sunrise, collected their manna, baked their daily bread and then packed a travel bag with enough sustenance to last for what was going to be a long day.

"What shall I wear?" asked Noah, as she tried yet another robe around her shoulders, "Do you think this will look good?" She did not wait for an answer, but shook her head and tossed the robe to the floor. "Can I wear your red one, Mahlah?"

They did not have many garments to choose from, but still making the decisions took up time that Hoglah felt they did not have, considering the lengthy walk ahead of them. Tension was mounting, but Milcah was ready with her natural diplomacy: "Noah, you looked fantastic in that blue shawl—try it on again." She draped it over Noah's shoulders, "Oh, yes, that's definitely *the best one for you. You look wonderful!*"

When they were all finally ready, Mahlah solemnly declared, "It's time to go. Come, sisters."

APPROACHING THE TENT OF MEETING

Today, to be granted audience with the Queen of England, you would first go before the community council, secondly to your Member of Parliament, then on to the House of Lords before ending up talking to the queen—if you were able to get that far. It might well have been more of a procedure, so many years ago, for the sisters to get to Moses—unless they timed it for an occasion like the census.

For events like this, all levels of government would have been present at the "city gates"—in front of the tent of meeting. Certainly, the young sisters went before three levels of leadership: the community leaders, the princes of the land, who had judiciary responsibilities including looking after the fatherless, then the priesthood and Moses himself.

> They stood before Moses and before Eleazar the priest and before the leaders and all the congregation, at the doorway of the tent of meeting.
> —NUMBERS 27:2, NASB

However, the sisters achieved their goal to meet with Moses, it would have been a feat. To begin with, it would be a long walk. In a camp of over two million people, the Zelo's tent might not have been as close to a perimeter as some, but to reach the tabernacle, it would still take them the best part of the morning. And they had to get there at least by lunchtime: their father's name was on the roll for some time in the afternoon, and what could be worse than missing their call? Also, for all the walking they had done in their lives, the path ahead of them was a very different kind of walk, needing all the courage they could muster.

The Hebrew camps were arranged in specific order

around the tabernacle. Immediately surrounding all four walls of the tabernacle were tents of the Levite clans. Then radiating out from there, north, south, east and west, were the four other camps—Ox camp, Lion camp, Eagle camp and Man camp. Each of these camps had three tribes living under its banner, according to the mother they shared in Jacob's family. When Moses was up the mountain and surveyed the vast campsite below, the land would have been stamped with an enormous cross pointing out to the four corners of the world. The daughters of Zelophehad would have lived somewhere on the section of the "cross" pointing westwards. Their walk would have taken them through the tents of their Ox camp into the Levites' domain, and thus to the tabernacle. Let us imagine the scene.

It is a spectacle for the women. They stand at tent doors, some with babies at their hips, chatting, laughing or pointing as they watch the men of warring age walking proudly towards the tent of meeting. The sisters set a steady pace, keeping their heads down. Young Tirzah, each step an anxious one, takes Mahlah's hand and holds it tightly.

"It's alright, Tirzah," whispers Mahlah, "no one will know we're not Levite women. Just keep walking."

So they walk on, keeping close, mostly in silence, weaving their way through groups of men. Their feet are already sore when they reach the boundary of the Levite tents, but at least they are more than halfway and making good time. More onlookers, more children running around, women pounding manna, men lighting fires and the air filled with the aroma of freshly baked bread…then suddenly, in front of them—the tent of meeting— closer than they have ever been before to the Holy Place. The glory cloud hovering just above the tabernacle, rising into the sky beyond sight; the sound of bleating sheep, ready for sacrifice; the fragrance of burning incense as it drifts over from the Holy Place. The air is thick, their hearts beat faster, their legs become heavy and their minds race with questions. Is this how their father used to feel on the rare occasions he had been here, alone, to make an offering? Are they going to be able to go through with it?

The sisters turn the corner and are now at the entrance side of the tent of meeting. People who lived in the vicinity, well used to being so close to the Holy Place, are coming and going; priests are busy grouping the Manasseh men into single file; Levite women are offering water to those who, unlike Zelophehad's daughters, had not come prepared for a long wait.

The girls make no attempt to join the line, but inch towards the tabernacle entrance, staying on the fringes of the merging men folk. They keep a careful eye on who is where, concealing themselves from uncles and cousins by drawing their shawls around their faces. They see the men filing past long tables, handing in their obligatory shekel as their numbers are recorded. Finally they see, seated on a low platform, the legal assembly, the tribal princes, Eleazar, the high priest—and Moses himself.

FACING THE CROWD

Names of the clans were being read out. From where they were up to, Mahlah knew Hepher, her family, was soon to be called. They had made it in time. She took Tirzah by the hand and pressed through the line of men, the other sisters joining them, in a single movement removing their shawls and revealing their presence. Their timing was perfect. Before anyone realized what was happening, Hepher's name and then Zelophehad's was called. Mahlah immediately stepped forward, and with a loud voice declared, "Our father died in the wilderness…"

A stunned silence fell on the crowd. It lasted only a few seconds. Scribes looked up from their bookkeeping, staggering to see five beautiful young ladies before them—very young, why, one of them barely into her teens. But Mahlah was the eldest, the tallest and the one obviously with the most authority. She stood there, feeling every eye boring into her—princes, priests, community leaders, Moses himself.

"What are these teenagers doing hanging around? They
don't look like Levite daughters."

"Girls! At the entrance to the tent of meeting!"

"Five of them!"

"What are they after?"

"Are they crazy?"

"They have no right to be here!"

"How did they get past the security men?"

Arms reached out to pull the girls away, but Moses, captivated by their boldness, raised an arm and said, "No—let
them speak."

Facing Moses

The girls had practiced their lines many times. But now, with
their hearts racing and their legs like jelly, it felt so very different. They stood in line, facing Moses, and each one delivered
one line of their appeal.

"Our father died in the wilderness without leaving any
sons," Mahlah finished, loudly and clearly.

"He was not among the followers of Korah, who rebelled
against the Lord." Another voice rang out.

"Korah died because of his own sin. Our father died of natural causes." As each girl spoke, her voice was stronger and
bolder than the one before.

"Just because our father had no sons, why should his name
disappear from Israel?"

Then it was Tirzah's turn. She took a deep breath, handed
over five shekels to a clerk, and confidently stated their request,

"We respectfully petition you to grant us the property
among our father's relatives that we believe is legally ours."

The clerk hurled the shekels to the ground as around them
the sound of agitated male voices swelled. Moses, undisturbed
by the commotion around him, stroked his long white beard and
considered. He was a wise man and he knew the law, but this
request was a new one to him. He surveyed the girls. They were

not only beautiful, but also upright in carriage, and had clear eyes that looked directly into his. They seemed nervous, but that was understandable; theirs was a daring request. Still, Moses reasoned, they were bold and courageous and had not let their fears hold them back. Above all, their appeal seemed to be reasonable and within Levitical laws on property and marriage.

Again the leader raised his hand and waited for the murmuring to subside.

"I will consult the Lord on this matter."

FACING GOD

Moses and the high priest moved into tent of meeting. The high priest had under his breastplate a pocket containing the Urim and Thummin, small black and white stones.[1] If the stones pulled were all white, then the Lord's answer was yes, if all were black it was no, and if the stones were both black and white, then the Lord was not ready to speak on the matter. Moses posed the question, and Eleazar reached into his garment for the answer, withdrawing three stones. Together they reappeared at the gate with the Lord's answer.

In the few moments that Moses stood there, pausing before he gave the Lord's decree, there was no sound at all, not even a single bleat from a lamb or goat within the tabernacle. The glory cloud was motionless and there was no shuffle of feet or garments amongst the crowd. The only movement was the trembling of the girls. Moses had handed down decrees before—hard ones—ones that had meant death.

But this was not one of those times. After Moses had finished, Mahlah fell onto her knees and wept tears of joy in the sand, three others joined hands and leaped around in a circle, and young Tirzah raised her hands to her face and fell to the ground in a swoon of relief. Some older women, who knew about such things, rushed to her aid, finding competition from a young prince who seemed to think she needed his strong helping hands. If any of the other men were expressing dissatisfaction, they could not be heard for the thousands of women who sent up a resounding cheer. Tirzah soon came to, meeting Moses' smile as he towered above her.

Composure regained, she whispered, "Thank you, sir," over and over again. Then she and her sisters collected themselves and quietly disappeared into the crowd.

Moses moved towards the census table and asked the scribe to move aside. This was one entry he wanted to write personally:

> Now Zelophehad the son of Hepher had no sons, but only daughters; and the names of the daughters of Zelophehad were Mahlah, Noah, Hoglah, Milcah and Tirzah.
> —NUMBERS 26:33, NASB

That night, Moses scrunched his robe into a makeshift pillow and lay down, his heart at peace with the decisions he had made. It had been a long, exhausting day, but the results were good—the tribes of Jacob had all survived, and thus far in the census process, it was obvious that a few, like Manasseh, had thrived and were now receiving their reward.

"Manasseh," he thought to himself, "a remarkable tribe indeed." The men in that tribe were fearsome warriors, but this was his first encounter with their gentler gender. The old man smiled when their five faces returned to his mind. Something about them reminded him of his older sister.

"Ah, Miriam," he whispered to himself, "what a plucky one you were. And beautiful, too!"

He pondered her bravery and how, as a young woman, she kept popping up throughout his childhood at the palace, always flashing a smile and darting off before she was caught away from her chores. He knew who she was—his adoptive mother often talked of how he had been found and then the slave girl's boldness. Then when he returned to his boyhood home years later, to face a new pharaoh, he was happy to see that Miriam still had a sparkle in her eyes and a winning way with words. "But then again, Lord, her words also often landed her in trouble."

A warm forgiveness settled quickly on the fading memories of her rebellious days. There was no doubt he missed her, probably mostly for her songs. While women generally were content to stay in the background, Miriam would at any time appear out there in front, delivering a prophetic song. Her normal voice was soft and sweet, no different than most women's, but when she struck up a prophetic song, a strength came into her voice, and things in the heavenlies seemed to snap like firecrackers, the fire in her voice blazing a trail that others could not help but follow.

Moses had had glimpses of that same fire in the eyes of those girls. He smiled to himself. It was not often, after so many years of teaching the law, that someone posed a question that he didn't know the answer to—never mind a woman.

"Ah, Lord, Zipporah would have enjoyed knowing these young ones." His wife had been one of seven sisters. The daughters of Jethro were no man's fools. In Moses' shepherding years, many a night was spent around a campfire, listening to them carry their own in debates with their husbands.

"Yes," mused Moses, "Zipporah would certainly have been interested in their cause." Still, he knew that even had she still been alive, he would not have discussed the case with her, or with Miriam, or with anyone else. Yes, tonight others would be sitting around in their tents discussing the sisters' plea, the minutiae of the law and the consequences of his rulings, but what others thought or said was of little concern to him. The Lord had instructed him to take difficult cases directly to Him; he had faithfully done so, received the answer and delivered it.

Moses placed his hands behind his head and released a contented sigh. As he lay there, he recalled the young faces, so innocent and yet so courageous, and tried to put a name to each. The little one, who was she? Yes, that's right, Tirzah.

"Something special about Tirzah," he said softly. "In fact, there's something special about the whole lot."

Lot—the word reminded him of the census and his weariness.

*He knew he would be seeing lots in his dreams, and there would
be no need to count sheep to get to sleep.*

QUALITIES OF A DAUGHTER OF ZELOPHEHAD

Moses was a man of true humility, more concerned about
God's honor than defending his position of power, staking
out his block or instinctively guarding male rights. The
matter of the daughters of Zelophehad was the last concern
he had to deal with before handing over leadership. Since
his father-in-law had advised him to delegate, Moses had
only dealt with two civilian affairs or family matters, apart
from his own. Both involved the daughters of
Zelophehad—young women of great character.

The daughters were just the kind of people the Lord was
looking for at the end of a desert season. The girls, in spite
of their differences and no doubt their weaknesses, had
many strengths in common. Let's bring them all together
and see what makes a daughter of Zelophehad.

BOLD COURAGE

The only male presence and the strength the girls had
drawn from so consistently was gone. Their father was dead
and with him his line. Every other family seemed to be
invited to the "lot party" except them. Did they really need
to go sticking their necks out when a simple romantic
attachment would solve their future homelessness problem?
That would be easier than trying to redefine property law.
No, they did not settle for the easiest route—the daughters
of Zelophehad chose a more courageous path.

But before making a move, there was a time of preparation. The girls had been brought up during hard times.
They had learned from the older generation's mistakes and
saw how those with courage and faith had been blessed,

while those without were not. The journey into the new land was not for the foolhardy or fainthearted, it was for those who knew their God.

> Be strong and of good courage, do not fear nor be afraid of them; for the LORD your God, He is the One who goes with you, He will not leave you nor forsake you.
> —DEUTERONOMY 31:6, NKJV

The daughters did not accept the way things had always been, nor were they intimidated by the fact that what they had in mind had never been done before. Yes, it may well be strange and new, difficult, perhaps even dangerous up ahead, but if the Lord says, "Go into that land" then courage dares His people to give it a go.

Some people are born pluckier than others, but Christian courage is not impulsive boldness or foolhardiness that steps out blindly and takes unnecessary risks. It is having a stout heart, grown over time, fed by the Word of God and the encouragement of others.

We develop courage when we face our fears—without a scary situation, who needs courage? Satan is the lion with bad breath, who breathes fear and discouragement over us. He wants us to see the grasshoppers as giants and wants his lies, and not God's truth, to determine the boundaries of our inheritance. But we know the other lion, the Lion of Judah, the one who gives us inspired lion-hearted courage. He not only sees us through our fear, but drives it out. Then we can move in with confidence and courage to take the inheritance God has already planned for us. The limits imposed by society concerning the sisters' inheritance rights were not from God. He was waiting for the girls to ask so that they could receive. How many things concerning our own inheritance have we not asked for and therefore not received?

Perhaps you are thinking, "Well, I am not bold or courageous. I feel weak, inadequate and just cannot do it!"

The Lord understands.

> We have not an high priest which cannot be touched
> with the feeling of our infirmities; but was in all
> points tempted like as we are, yet without sin. [He
> knows the feelings that oppress us and possess us.] Let
> us therefore come boldly unto the throne of grace,
> that we may obtain mercy, and find grace to help in
> time of need.
>
> —Hebrews 4:16, kjv

Whatever help we need, the Lord has it parceled up and ready for us—when we are ready to take it.

Our daughter, Shaeron, also did a course with Youth With a Mission (YWAM), based here in Perth and then three months overseas. Initially, she was not far from us, but she struggled with terrible homesickness. This caught us all, including our independent seventeen-year-old, by surprise; after all, she had flown across the world before without us, been in boarding school for a season and loved both adventures.

The night before she was due to leave on outreach to China and Thailand, Shaeron called in tears, not knowing if she should still go. We headed off to bring her home, but when we arrived, there was no need. A guest speaker had prayed for her and Shaeron received the assurance from the Lord that she was on the right track. She went off the next day, still tearful, but prepared to trust the Lord with her concerns.

She had some great experiences, but also faced long train rides, rat-infested rooms, enforced moves by the police (to a better, safer hotel), diarrhea and sickness. I wondered if she would ever have the nerve to go so far away from us again, but within a month she was off to work in orphanages in India and Romania, this time without the added security of a team. She faced some very hard situations, including being stranded at an airport in the aftermath of the September 11 terrorist attacks, but she came through them all because courage and tenacity had been worked into her character.

CHARACTER OF A DAUGHTER OF ZELOPHEHAD

RIGHTEOUS CHALLENGE

The daughters of Zelophehad, as offspring of Abraham, issued an unexpected challenge to place the Abrahamic promise under their feet.

> And I will establish My covenant between Me and you and your descendants after you in their generations, for an everlasting covenant, to be God to you and your descendants after you. Also I give to you and your descendants after you the land in which you are a stranger, all the land of Canaan, as an everlasting possession; and I will be their God.
> —GENESIS 17:7–8, NKJV

The daughters learned the promises of God and held them close to their hearts. They wanted to be part of the covenant; they believed their father's land was rightfully theirs and, believing it could be, challenged the traditional interpretation of the laws of their land.

Moses faced many challenges, not all legitimate: Pharaoh challenged Moses and lost his son, Miriam wrongly confronted her brother and lost her health, the woodcutter defied the Sabbath laws and lost his life, and then, of course, there was Korah.

When the ten spies were issued a challenge in Canaan, eight of them took it in the wrong way and paid for it. Jolted by the Lord's pronouncement that none of that generation would see the new land, reactionaries decided to take the land challenge and headed for the hills, but they acted presumptuously, going without God's blessing, timing and help. It might have been the right challenge, but it was at the wrong time and in the wrong spirit. The penalty for this was death.

The daughters of Zelophehad challenged the law in the right spirit, saw big changes take place as a result and lived. It was no easy challenge. Firstly, there was the challenge concerning their father's name, then the challenge of womanhood and finally the challenge of care for orphans in

183

their distress. All three challenges are ones the Lord loves to hear and respond to when done in the right spirit.

FRUITFUL FAITH

> Without faith it is impossible to please God.
> —HEBREWS 11:6, NIV

God was pleased with these women. They may have offended some in the camp, but they did not offend the Lord. Daring faith is reproductive; it produces fruit, and because the changes in the law were for everyone, the daughters of Zelophehad unknowingly sowed seed for women of all time.

Our desert situations may look as if they are sandy infertile places, but as we plod on through them, scattering even mustard seed amounts of faith, we will see them transformed into places of vibrant growth.

What is it that God is asking us to have faith for? Is there some work that we must do to exercise our faith muscles? There is a long list in heaven of the Accounts of Faith, an extended version of Hebrews 11; by faith Moses, by faith Joshua, by faith Mahlah, Noah, Milcah, Hoglah and Tirzah. Everyone on that list faced a hard situation and then demonstrated their faith in action. By faith, you and I. If you are facing the hardest situation you have ever had to face in your life, then take heart—entry into the Accounts of Faith list is based on our life's hardest moment and our response to it.

> Dear brothers and sisters, what's the use of saying you
> have faith if you don't prove it by your actions?
> —JAMES 2:14, NLT

UNITING LOVE

For the sisters, it was all for one, and one for all. They shared a common inheritance, and it was therefore important they move together, encouraging one another to walk on. United they would stand; divided they would fall. They survived, but more than that—they thrived.

We will thrive too, when we are connected to the right people. The kingdom is about relationships, how we connect with God, with one another and with the communities we live in.

Unity is important at many different levels, but it always starts with individuals and will be frequently tested. We need unity in our homes, unity between our friends and in our churches, and, let's not forget, unity of churches within a city and nation.

Five girls walked in unity and saw laws transformed. Five families walking in unity would make a wonderful home group, five churches a splendid network of cooperation in our cities, and five nations working together—what a force to contend with that would be!

It is not easy to get people to live and work together. It means laying down control, personal agendas and ambitions so that we can see the others grow. The church is not a business; it is a family, bonded in love. Love is our unity glue that makes people sit up and notice that we have something special to say.

> By this all will know that you are My disciples, if you have love for one another.
> —JOHN 13:35, NKJV

The daughters were connected by their love for their father, and that's the bottom line for us too.

INSPIRED VISION

The daughters of Zelophehad had a vision, as crazy as it seemed at the time: they believed for their father's inheritance. They saw God's justice and character reflected in their laws, and they were prepared to act upon the vision they were given. Their vision was indeed in line with the Father heart of God. Their vision had repercussions beyond themselves. It included the potential for a society that cared better for its orphaned daughters and people caught in the margins of society because of circumstances beyond their control.

Many people have a vision but do nothing about it. My friend, Julie, was given a vision that seemed so crazy, we knew it had to be God. It was risky, bold and radical. The Lord told her to gather the churches together to announce a year of jubilee over her entire city—debt cancellation for a whole city. (I touched on this earlier, in chapter five.) So that is what she did, and that is what the churches did in response. Over the space of only a few months, they raised more than enough money to pay off the debts of some of the poorest people in Fremantle, port city to Perth, the capital of Western Australia. For one week, water bills, gas bills, rent and electricity were paid, those facing eviction from their homes were told their debts had been paid in full, and yet others were given free hot dogs, water bottles and car washes. This very tangible demonstration of the love of Christ was well registered by utilities boards, the mayor and the media. What a lesson for them on how Jesus releases us from the debt of sin!

ENTERPRISING INITIATIVE

Another strong character the girls displayed was initiative. They didn't wait for someone else to come up with a solution to their problem or hope that another might take the risks on their behalf. No, they made the decision to be counted and were enterprising enough to secure their inheritance. Their lives counted for far more than they would ever have realized. One day, one decision—changing lives, and inspiring others, even until today.

We never know when we take an initiative just how much fruit it will bear. I wonder if Loren Cunningham of Youth With a Mission or George Verwer of Operation Mobilisation would ever have guessed when they started out how many young people would take up the challenge to missions through their respective organizations. They stepped out in faith with what they had at the time, and the Lord blessed their efforts and then expanded their vision bit by bit until both organizations became global in their impact. As the old Chinese proverb says, "a journey of a thousand miles begins with the first step." God is looking for those who will be enterprising enough to take that first step.

PATIENT HUMILITY

The girls didn't rush in immediately after their father's death but waited for the right moment, a *kairos* or opportune time. This would have taken patience. There is a time to keep a low profile and a time to stand up and be counted. For the girls, that time was the census.

The word *census* means "lifting up one's head."

> But You, O Lord, are a shield for me, my glory and the One who lifts up my head.
>
> —PSALM 3:3, NKJV

We must be patient for the desert to do its work, but when the Lord says it is a time to stand up and be counted, to lift our heads, then it's time to go forward. There is no attitude of pride or haughtiness in lifting up our heads. In fact, "Canaan" is a place for those who are humble. Canaan means "low land" and comes from a word meaning "to be brought low, or humbled."

Lifted heads and humble hearts, walking in the graceful steps of patience, are great traits for moving forward in God.

HONORING AND RESPECTFUL WOMEN

Commotion and boisterous demonstrations can get a hearing with people of influence, but the daughters chose neither.

They displayed respect for God's Ten Commandments when they sought their father's honor.

> Children, obey your parents in the Lord, for this is right. "Honor your father and mother," which is the first commandment with promise: "that it may be well with you and you may live long on the earth."
> —EPHESIANS 6:1–3, NKJV

The girls' desire to honor their father was way beyond their desire for land. That is the way it must be with us too; this is not about making a name for ourselves, but making a name for our Father in heaven. Any ministries or ideas birthed as a result of our courage and initiative must be about honoring Him and not us, or they are doomed to eventual failure. We must be about our Father's business. When He calls, we listen; when He sends, we go. The girls, unlike Korah, did not dishonor their government or leadership when they took their stand.

And the way they conducted themselves was in fine manner. They were not rude or arrogant but respectful and honorable.

Wise and Righteous Speech

Not only was the girls' manner respectful, what they spoke was true and the Lord upheld their appeal.

> The daughters of Zelophehad speak what is right.
> —NUMBERS 27:7, NKJV

God affirms that their boldness was based on a just cause. They knew and understood enough of the law to know they had a good case—reflecting God's heart for the poor. Speaking what is right requires understanding and knowledge, but it also calls for wisdom.

Wisdom is more than just being right; knowledge alone can give that. Wise speech is seasoned with grace and righteousness. (See Colossians 4:4.)

> The mouth of the righteous brings forth wisdom.
> —PROVERBS 10:31, NKJV

Righteous people, those in right relationship with God, open their mouths and wisdom pours out. Wisdom does not just affect our speech—our hearts are stirred to use our gifts and talents to glorify God.

> And all the women whose hearts stirred with wisdom spun yarn of goats' hair.
> —EXODUS 35:26, NKJV

The wise women, even in their desert days, spun long, silken goats' hair to make a luxurious fabric for use in the tabernacle.[2] This nanny goat, *ez*, comes from a root meaning "strong, prevailing and firm." Those who are wise in speech and action will be unshakeable, their lives spinning a protective covering for themselves and a tabernacle for God to inhabit.

The daughters of Zelophehad knew the law well enough to know they have reason to be covered by it. Their plea was fivefold and ingenious:

> Our father died.
> He did not rebel.
> He died because of his own sin.
> We want to honor his name.
> Give us his inheritance.

Their argument was simple, honest and well-reasoned. Compare their appeal with ours based on the life of Christ:

> Jesus died for us.
> He did not rebel once.
> He died for our sin.
> We honor his name.
> We share in his inheritance.

Desert to Destiny

When David sang Psalm 68, he might have been thinking about the daughters of Zelophehad. Why? Well, he sang about the Lord being a father to the fatherless, a defender of widows and setting the solitary in families. The setting of the psalm was the desert, transformed by the abundant rain of God.

> You, O God, sent a plentiful rain, whereby You con-firmed Your inheritance …You, O God, provided from Your goodness for the poor. The Lord gave the word; great was the company of those who proclaimed it. Kings of armies flee…And she who remains at home divides the spoil.
> —Psalm 68:9–12, NKJV

In this verse "company" is gender specific—this is about women. True daughters of Zelophehad are those who, even in their desert seasons smell the coming inheritance rains and wisely proclaim the Word of the Lord, sending the enemy fleeing.

Godly Obedience

Remember the girls' names all end with a contraction for the name Jehovah? Zelophehad could well have named them with the very intention of reminding his daughters they belonged to Jahweh. But bearing God's name, or any other man-given title, is not enough to get people to their destiny. The bearer must also display His nature. They must be godlike or godly. Godliness comes from spending time with the Lord, learning who He is, listening to what He says—and then, because we love Him, we obey Him. As we will later see, the girls' volun-tarily obeyed the Lord's commands concerning their inheritance, putting the needs of their tribe before their own rights to choose a partner from wherever they wanted. Without that obedience, they would see the Promised Land, but not the full extent of their own inheritance.

Being godly is not following a religious code or creed.

Jesus called the most religious people of His day, the Pharisees, hypocrites and whitewashed tombs, outwardly beautiful but inside just a pile of rotting bones. (See Matthew 23:27.)

Being godly is not about devotion to a cause—devout women ran Paul and Barnabas out of town. (See Acts 13:50.) We can be totally committed to religion and causes and miss out on relationship. It takes a solid relationship with a person to really become like them—God included. And because God knows what is best for us and gives us instructions to live by, for our own good, obedience to Him is a vital attribute for those who want to see their inheritance.

FRUIT AND FLOWERS OF THE DESERT

When all these attributes of a daughter of Zelophehad are put together, a person is well on his way to being godly and godlike, displaying the fruit of His Spirit. God is courageous, challenging, faithful, righteous, wise and much more. And it is in the desert days that He grows His people's understanding of who He is. The desert days grow daughters of Zelophehad. They are those whose eyes are no longer on the old structures of Goshen, but have had them refocused through the transitional, wilderness days to know that God cares for them and can be trusted to take care of them, too. The desert has blossomed under His nurture, and in Zelophehad's case, produced five lovely roses.

The journey back to their tent seemed shorter than the one they had taken that morning, but even so the sisters did not reach home until well after sundown. It was not a walk in darkness: the light from the pillar of fire softly illuminated the whole camp, even to its farthest borders. But to the girls, it seemed to shine brighter that night than on any other night they could remember.

Along the path they were greeted with many smiles and congratulations. Had there been any negative comments, Mahlah, Noah, Hoglah, Milcah and young Tirzah would not have noticed. They entered their tent, footsore and weary, but hearts ablaze with joy. Tonight, sleep. Tomorrow, celebration.

They did not know it, but there was one test still remaining—and this test would come from within their own family.

CHAPTER 10

Family Matters

*Then the heads of the clan of Gilead—
descendants of Makir, son of Manasseh, son of
Joseph—came to Moses and the family leaders of
Israel with a petition.*

—NUMBERS 36:1, NLT

M oses thought it would not be long before he had another
visit from the tribe of Manasseh. He was not wrong.
Eleazar announced that a delegation from the girls' clan, the
Gileadites, wanted an audience.

"And in what spirit do they come, Eleazar?" asked Moses,
authority etched in his voice.

"Sir, they come in the same manner as the young women
did—with reverence and boldness in their eyes."

"Good," responded Moses, nodding as he continued, "an
answer to my prayers." Then he was silent. Eleazar waited
patiently. Moses was not one who rushed into things without
consulting the Lord. Some days the high priest felt Moses'
silences lasted for hours, but today it was only a long, pregnant
pause before the great leader spoke again. Eleazar released his
breath in relief.

"Gather all the tribal princes. Bring the Manasseh clan

leaders forward."

This contingent from Manasseh was very different. Whereas the girls had come with just one another for support, their cousins and uncles had come en masse. This time it seemed the entire tribe of Manasseh was standing on Levite soil with their clan leaders, resolute, at the head. The girls were there too, having been instructed to come along, as if they were evidence. They stood quietly and this time did not utter a word.

"Sir, concerning the daughters of Zelophehad," their spokesman began, reading from a scroll and gesturing towards the girls for effect, "we in Manasseh know the Lord has given His decree on the matter of their plea and they have been awarded a portion of land. But we, their fellow tribesmen, are concerned that our land will be depleted should they marry outside our tribe."

Moses knew the issue was centered on the new jubilee laws concerning redistribution of land every fifty years. In the next breath another Gileadite clan leader spoke that out.

"Well, at least they know the law," thought Moses to himself, "and their request seems reasonable, but I had better be sure..."

"I will seek the Lord's mind on this matter," Moses said, turning back with Eleazar towards the entrance to the tent of meeting. Most of the people chose to wait, as if instinctively knowing Moses would not be long. The Gileadites sat around discussing whether they had put their case clearly enough, wondering if Moses would represent them properly before God and what His answer might be. Before long, their leader reappeared, with the high priest and Joshua at his side. The people immediately stood up quietly and gathered in front of him.

Moses paused, noticing there was not the same anxiety in the air. "Their confidence in the Lord is increasing, Joshua," Moses whispered. "Can you see it on their faces?"

Between the two visits from Manasseh, Moses had been up the mountain and had seen the land the Lord was giving to the people. His time on earth was nearing an end. He had already handed over some responsibilities to Joshua and taught him strategic warfare lessons during the Midianite battles. Moses was becoming increasingly aware that God's chosen people were ready to move into their land. His voice boomed out over them.

"Hear, O Israel, the Lord has spoken on the matter." Moses looked at the clan leaders before him and saw, written on their faces, submission and expectancy. "Manasseh, you have asked well, just as your nieces and cousins, the daughters of Zelophehad, did before you." He turned to the five young girls and addressed them directly, keeping his voice raised, and speaking slowly.

"Now, daughters of Zelophehad, you may marry anyone you please." Moses could hear his words echoing as others repeated the words for those out of earshot. A few of the young cousins looked dismayed as they waited for Moses to continue, but most retained expressions of anticipation.

"However, in order to keep the land within your tribe, you must find a husband from within your father's clan." The girls nodded with understanding, and the men breathed a sigh of relief.

Moses called for the law books to be taken to his personal tent for amendment. Then he cast one last look at the young women who had so daringly requested the changes. They were walking away arm in arm, the dispersing crowds making way for them as they went.

"Yes, Lord," he whispered to the heavens, "these men and women are ready to take the land." For a long time, Moses had waited to see people with the courage and faith of Joshua and Caleb, those who displayed a reverence towards the Lord. Now Manasseh's people had modeled that for a new generation.

The leader, now one hundred and twenty years old, knew his job was done. He had just one more real mountain to climb. Even for his age, he was strong and he knew he would take it in stride. Moses was glad his eyesight was still perfect. That meant, even from the mountaintop, he would see land as far as any man and then, having glimpsed it, he could rest in peace.

DAUGHTERS OF INFLUENCE

The daughters of Zelophehad not only had an impact on their extended family members. Their action also had an effect on their clan and on the whole Hebrew community. No one could ignore them or what they had achieved, whether they liked it or not.

Their cousins and uncles might, at first reading, seem to be protecting their own assets, but the Gileadite's case was bold, reasonable and focused on the honor of their forefather, Manasseh. The Lord said they spoke "rightly," just as the daughters had done. Both men and women had a firm grasp of the laws concerning the land; the women understood the Lord's care and concern for widows and orphans in distress, the men had grasped the jubilee laws and how land was to be kept within a tribe. God's inheritance was for both men and women, each bringing a different and important aspect into the picture. Up until now, this had not been of concern to anyone, but now it was: before the Jordan could be crossed, closing the gap between desert and destiny, the gender gap also had to be crossed.

After the visit of their family to Moses, the spirit of the daughters of Zelophehad could be seen to be multiplying. Doing things the right way, after seeking God's opinion, gave far better results than grumbling, complaining or setting up a rebellion. The whole experience had been a powerful example of the importance of listening to God, listening to their leader, listening to each other. Not only was Manasseh's tribe blessed through the daughters' achievement, women of any tribe, in similar situations, could now also receive an inheritance.

Their influence did not stop there. Down through the ages their spirit has persisted, inspiring women to action. The daughters of Zelophehad might not be well known to many in our churches today, but we don't have to look far to see a daughter who has carved out a destiny not only for herself, but also for others, through her courage and persistence against all odds.[1]

Early church history is full of accounts of remarkable women. Take Marcella (325–410), a teacher in the early church in Rome, whose palatial home became a place of deep discussion, study, prayer and concern for the community. Marcella lived in a society where the rich flaunted their wealth, but she dressed simply and used her wealth to aid the poor. Her affluent upbringing did not spare her desert seasons; her father had died when she was a child, and she was widowed at just seventeen. Marcella inspired other women to take up their own call: Fabiola began Rome's first hospital; a mother and daughter team, Paula and Eustochium, went with Jerome to Bethlehem to translate the Bible into Latin. As if she was not busy enough, Paula pioneered a hospice and two monasteries—all because her friend Marcella, understanding her godly inheritance, opened up her home and her heart.[2]

In England, Hannah More (1745–1833) was, like the Zelos, one of five sisters. Her three older sisters, while still in their teens, began a boarding school, and Hannah completed her education there. By seventeen she had published her first book and had become well known for her literary skills. During her life, Hannah used her gifts to write about spiritual and moral issues for everyone, rich and poor, to read. She enjoyed strong friends: John Newton, her pastoral advisor and William Wilberforce, who inspired her to oppose slavery, poverty and illiteracy. She had her desert seasons, three times being left at the altar, but chose not to live in bitterness and used her talents to benefit others. Later, when the five More sisters began a Sunday school reaching more than twenty thousand children, much of the literature used was written by Hannah.[3]

We can only presume these women, well educated in the Bible, would have read the story of the daughters of Zelophehad. One group definitely well acquainted with the daughters was the suffragettes of the early twentieth century. These women began to rise up around the globe, including Canada, America, Britain and Australia, and demand the legal right to inherit, to vote and to stand in political office.

Around this time, women did not have inheritance rights, and the suffragettes campaigned vigorously over this issue, often using the daughters' example to back their case. Not all men were unsupportive: in 1913, an address given to Women's Clubs by Chief Justice Walker Clark mentions the daughters' story when commenting on the tardiness of the North Carolina courts to give land rights to women.[4]

In 1927 in Canada, five Christian women, the "famous five," changed history when they petitioned the Supreme Court to allow women to be appointed to the Senate. Their first request failed, but Irene, Emily, Nellie, Henrietta and Louise, each a successful campaigner in her own right, did not give up. They appealed and two years later won their case, opening a door for women to political positions of influence.[5]

And the daughters' influence continues today. Although many in today's generation have not heard of the daughters of Zelophehad, they are not forgotten, being held as models of boldness for groups such as the Young Women's Christian Association.

> As far back as 1914, as the then World's Committee met to focus on the future, a YWCA leader from Sweden, Anna Roos, called upon the movement to find within its ranks "daughters of Zelophehad," who would have the courage and forthrightness to "speak right," to claim their place in the congregation of their brethren, and thereby claim also the possibility of leadership. Whenever there was oppression, Anna Roos declared, there was also the opportunity for daughters of Zelophehad to emerge. Opportunity—and challenge—for as the Book of Numbers tells their story, these bold daughters had to have the strength not to fight for their own rights, but to seek justice for

all the oppressed of the world. It was a call, on the eve of the First World War, for the YWCA to take national and international responsibility...At Cairo in this summer of 1999, as at all Councils of years past, the world movement will renew and reaffirm its dedication to world peace and justice—and create the wonderful moment for new daughters of Zelophehad to step forward, lift the twin-flamed torch, and bear it forth.[6]

—RAZIA ISMAIL ABBASI, WORLD YWCA PRESIDENT
1991–1995

This story from the Bible is not about championing women's rights, where women win and men lose. And it is not about women winning some rights and men fighting to regain power and control. It is about what God wants—His law, His will and His way. Since it was never God's will for women, marginalized or otherwise, to be left destitute, then it was piety and not feminism that caused the daughters of Zelophehad to speak. And God's will was for their influence to multiply and bear fruit down through the ages.

That is not to say the Bible has nothing to say about the rights or treatment of women—Jesus radically challenged the cultural and religious views concerning women in His time. He treated women, whether His mother, a young girl, a prostitute or social outcast, with the same level of justice and love as He displayed towards men. (See John 4; Mark 16:9.)

THE BORDERS OF OUR INHERITANCE

The daughters' actions may have caused some interesting reactions. After the first judgment came from the Lord, giving them their father's land, imagine the flurry of suitors arriving at their door, bearing gifts and seeking their hands in marriage. While that might have seemed a blessing, it might well have brought pressures on the girls as well.

"How can I chose from such a crowd?"

"Who will plan my wedding?"

"I wish Papa was here to help me!"

"If only my mother was here to make me my dress!"

The girls did not have a mother or father to match-make on their behalf, offer wise advice about the girls' romantic attachments or to arrange a dowry and a wedding. But they did have uncles who decided they needed a say.

The family intervention might, at first sight, seem to have brought the women to a place of confinement. However, the new restrictions could also be seen as a blessing, bringing their choice to a much more manageable level. The first amendment to the Law said: "Yes, you can have your land." The second gave the borders of the land of promise: "Marry within this field." Neither their inheritance, nor their freedom, was diminished by the Lord's instruction, just more clearly defined. And the Lord pointed out, when it comes to our inheritance, we do not function alone; family—His family—matters.

Every now and then the Lord gives us a specific word that our lives will bear much fruit. And as we hear it, we think, "Can this really be true? This seems too big, too vast to comprehend—how will it ever come to pass?" Well, it often happens in ways we could never imagine and always in ways that will delight us, enabling us to say, like David:

> The boundary lines have fallen for me in pleasant places, surely I have a delightful inheritance.
> —PSALM 16:5–6, NIV

We can be sure that, when we seek His wisdom, the Lord will give us progressive insight into our call, its field and its borders.

I saw this as a single person wondering about marriage. My calling was to missions, particularly the Far East, and so that narrowed down the field of choice for me. I imagined that would mean I would either remain single or marry a missions-minded Scot with a calling to the Chinese. I never anticipated I would marry a Chinese man from Borneo and set up home in a nation closed to conventional missionary work, placing me for many years in a wonderful mission field.

The daughters had a rich inheritance, more far-reaching than they would have dreamed of, yet it was found within borders and their obedience to God's commands. Marrying the right guys enabled the women to move from their deserts to their destinies.

Daughters of Double Blessing

"I can't believe it," giggled Milcah when they bedded down that night. "Did you see all those guys?"

"Did we see them?" quipped Hoglah, "They were bowing so low, they were practically wiping the dust off our feet!"

"And their chat-up lines?" added Milcah, "I've never had so many offers to escort me home before!"

"Or move into their homes!" groaned Mahlah.

"I've never seen so many eligible men all in one place at one time!" said Noah.

"Oh yes, and some not so eligible!" Hoglah added.

Tirzah hooted with laughter, remembering the man with a monstrous nose covered in warts who had commented on "what lovely eyes" she had. Mahlah reached over and stuffed a pillow into her sister's face to stop the squeals coming out.

"And what about those Machirites," said Tirzah, putting on a serious face and mocking them, "Sisters, we have a word from God for you—you are to be our wives!"

That was enough to set them all off, the exhilaration of the day giving way to momentary hysteria. Even Mahlah, usually the sensible and serious one, grabbed a cushion to stifle her glee. They had had enough attention for one day, and the last thing they needed now was one of the leaders coming around asking them to be quiet at such a late hour. Their voices may have been muffled, but their joy was not. Never before had the girls felt so deliriously happy, and it was made all the more fun with all these men hanging around smiling silly smiles that offered, "Marry me!"

The girls had become the talk of the town. These were "daughters of double blessing." Any Gileadite who married one of them would have a double inheritance. Every single man in the Manasseh camp knew exactly who they were, where their tent was and when they went to water their animals. Within a day the girls went from a position of vulnerability to one of extraordinary favor. They were now the five most eligible girls in their tribe and were enjoying the moment immensely.

CHAPTER 11

Taking the New Land

*Get ready to cross the Jordan River into the land I
am about to give to them—to the Israelites.*
—JOSHUA 1:2, NIV

Home for the daughters was now on the other side of the
Jordan. They had been camped at Gilgal for almost seven
years after the Crossing. What a day that had been, when the
river rolled back as far as the eye could see. Manna had long
since disappeared, ceasing after the first Passover in the new
land. Times were different now; food was plentiful, water fresh
and grazing good for the animals. Wars had been fought and
won, weddings planned, marriages consummated and
bouncing babies born.

Milcah was the last one to find a husband. All her sisters
had married in quick succession, and she was left to fend off
the remaining suitors. She wondered if she would ever leave
the family tent and find the man of her dreams. Yes, she had
plenty of offers, but none she wanted to accept. Then she also
found one who made her heart flutter, leaving the tent of
Zelophehad, for the first time ever, lifeless.

There had been no time before the wedding, but now the daughters of Zelophehad had a task they could no longer put off. They gathered in the tent for one last time. They stood inside the fondly familiar but now bare abode and stared at the patches on the fabric that covered the wooden frame.

"Like a rich tapestry, isn't it?" said Mahlah, remembering her mother protecting them from trickling rain and even howling sandstorms with her deft handiwork.

"Yes, just like our lives," agreed Noah, "lots of rough patches, but worth a great deal."

"How can life in a desert be so enriching, so rewarding?" Tirzah asked.

Noah nodded and smiled. "Yes, Tirzah, we've been so blessed." She picked up the one remaining item from the floor of the tent, an old clay lamp, and dusted it off gently, as if it was made of gold. This had been their mother's treasured item, booty from Egypt. The sisters had decided that Noah, who had been especially fond of the lamp, was to take it with her when the last of them left the tent.

"If tents had ears, then this one knows a lot of secrets," Hoglah said, making them chuckle, each with their own thoughts on the matter.

"Oh, I remember when you were born, Hoglah," Mahlah said. "You were the cutest little partridge." Then she turned to the youngest two sisters and said, "And both of you, too, I remember it just as if it was yesterday."

"Yes, who could forget Papa's joy at Tirzah's birth?" Noah rubbed her growing belly and wondered if she was carrying a girl or a boy. She was not the only one with child, but Hoglah had not yet discovered that she, too, was extending her borders, again.

Mahlah noticed Noah's affectionate stroking of the child within. "Noah, you'll soon be passing on Papa's stories." A wide grin spread over Noah's face as story time with their father came to mind.

"I'm ready."

"I'm sure you are—and I'm sure there'll be a few more babies born in this old tent before it's through," laughed Tirzah, *"but perhaps none like the daughters of Zelophehad!"*

It was a poignant moment. They were in no hurry to leave the tent. They sat in a circle and placed the lamp in the middle, just as they had so many times as children, then too, after their father died…After an hour or so a gentle breeze entered the tent. The sisters felt its presence and stopped talking. A quiet peace fell upon them. It was the same sweet wind that had touched them many times before.

"Let's trim the wick one more time together," Noah suggested quietly, breaking the silence. "For old time's sake."

They arose together and stood quietly in the center of the tent. With reverence, Noah held the lamp up for Mahlah who solemnly did the trimming and then placed it on the floor in front of them. They could almost hear their mother's voice echoing round the tent, *"Keep your wicks trimmed every day, girls, and your lamps will always shine brightly!"*

The sisters stood, holding hands, gazing at the lamp, each saying their own goodbyes to their childhood, to their tent home and to the desert.

"We should go," Mahlah said at last, choosing her words deliberately, "It's time, come girls." Farewells over, an important meeting lay ahead, this time not with Moses, but with Joshua.

The five sisters emerged to find their husbands walking towards them, tools in hand.

"Good timing," said Noah, smiling, her lamp secure in her hands. Before they knew it, the now-famous tent of Zelophehad was dismantled, and the five daughters of Zelophehad set off on another walk.

Meeting with Joshua

Zelophehad's daughters had received their promise, but, like everyone else, had to wait for it to come into effect. Some days, when a war was raging, they felt as if they would never see a permanent building on their own plot of land. But the daughters had no intention of giving up until they felt the soil of their promises under their feet.

Then came a peaceful period, and Joshua was finally ready to allot the land to each family.

The women were ready now too; if they had received their inheritance a few years previously, they might have collapsed under the weight of responsibility. With their husbands alongside and other new-found friends supporting them, they were mostly just excited with anticipation. A little voice somewhere at the back of their minds had whispered occasional doubts, but deep down they had known the God-given decree would come to fruition, one day. That day had finally come. The daughters arrived before Joshua in perfect timing for the allocation of land to Zelophehad's closest relatives.

> They went to Eleazar the priest, Joshua the son of Nun, and the leaders and said, "The Lord commanded Moses to give us an inheritance among our brothers."
> —JOSHUA 17:4, NIV

Eleazar looked older, Joshua too—seven years of war had taken a toll, but had not affected their memories. They recognized the women before they even opened their mouths to speak. Joshua did not retry the case or stall them or even consult the Lord—the Lord had already spoken—he simply nodded in agreement and handed the women five "tickets" to the lottery.

THE NATIONAL LOTTERY

Moses' lottery told them where each tribe was to war, but this one was about where each extended family would live. And the lot lay in the lap of the Lord. (See Proverbs 16:33.) There is nothing left to chance about anything in God's lap, and giving out land by lots, in this way, under God's authority, meant there would be less chance of stampedes, fighting and jealousy.

THE DAUGHTERS' LOT

So how much land did the daughters of Zelophehad receive, and where was it? Manasseh's lot was divided into two parts, fulfilling the prophetic action of Manasseh, Joseph's son, when he rent his garment in two, years before. (See Genesis 44:13.) This was not about Joseph's inheritance being divided into the two tribes of Manasseh and Ephraim, but about Manasseh itself dividing again two half tribes. One-half of Manasseh, led by Machirite warriors, inherited Gilead and Bashan, east of the Jordan. Two other tribes, Gad and Reuben, also chose to inherit on this eastern side because of the good grazing. The men from these two and a half tribes secured cities for their wives and children to live in, and then, as Moses had commanded, most crossed the Jordan to help the other nine and a half tribes win their land.

Although descendants of Machir, the daughters crossed over the Jordan to inherit in the east alongside the other half of Manasseh and the other nine tribes.

> And there fell ten portions to Manasseh, beside the land of Gilead and Bashan, which were on the other side Jordan.
> —JOSHUA 17:5, KJV

There were ten portions for this half of the tribe, five of which went to the daughters. Why were there ten portions? Well, their grandfather, Hepher, had five brothers and each received a portion, leaving five, one for each daughter. Although we do not know if the portions were of equal size, it was for the girls, quite possibly, a sizeable inheritance.

The Bible gives us some idea of where western Manasseh's land lay. Their lot was not only large, but also contained the best of all kinds of terrain, including trade seaports and life-giving rivers with good fishing. It stretched from the Great Sea (now the Mediterranean) to the river Jordan on the east. The southern boundary was the *Kanah Brook*, and in the north it extended inland from the Carmel range. (See Joshua 17; 19:26.) Manasseh included the Sharon, a thirty- to fifty-mile fertile coastal plain renowned for its beauty, thick oak forests and several cities.[1]

In addition, tribes were assigned a city within another tribal zone, ensuring some measure of communication between the "brothers." Manasseh was given a city within Issachar—Meggido, one of the largest and wealthiest walled cities.[2] Archaeologists have discovered that this city (now Tel Megiddo), had a gate, temple, palace and water supply system.[3] The New Testament mentions a place of the same name—*Armageddon*. In Jesus' time, most of western Manasseh's land was part of Samaria. Today it includes much of the disputed West Bank.

Interestingly, this area also contained *Tirzah*, the beautiful city mentioned in Song of Songs. Archaeological discoveries have positioned Tirzah at the end of a long, fertile valley, seven miles northeast of ancient Shechem, now Nablus.[4] Set on a hill, it had massive walls. Jereboam (926–909 B.C.) declared it capital of the Northern Kingdom of Israel, which it remained for forty years. (See Joshua 17:1–3; 1 Kings 14:17.)

"I can't believe it," said Tirzah to her husband, "we're here at last!"

"And now it's time to start building, my sweet little Tirz." Snuggled together on a large rock at the top of a hill, within earshot of their children sleeping in the tent below, the couple was enjoying a few quiet moments under the stars. They were considering the position of their first proper home. Unlike some, they had decided not to move into a house vacated by

their enemies—no, after all these years of dreaming, Tirzah was taking no easy way out. She had other house plans in mind, and her husband was only too willing to help her fulfill them.

A little farther downhill, Mahlah was rocking a child to sleep. She was tired. It had taken many days' walk to get from Gilgal to their new land.

"I'm not so sure I want to go off to war again, my dear, leaving you with all these little ones." People were keen to occupy their land, but the men were nonetheless nervous about having brought their wives and children to establish homes so close to cities not yet taken.

"We could do with a few more Machirites around here, Mahlah," he said, "they're the strongest warriors I've ever fought alongside."

Mahlah stroked her restless child's hair, thinking with pride about the mighty men of valor who were now heading back to the east, and looked up to smile at her husband. "But then, my love, we are from Machirite stock ourselves. It may seem a large task, but weak as we may feel, with Jahweh's help, we can do it."

Noah also was exhausted—from little sleep and constant feeding. Her baby was only a few weeks old when her clan had made the final move. So far, she had not told any of her Papa's stories to the child. He was much too young. And anyway, at the end of the day she had little energy left. Ah, at last he had settled. She turned over to get some sleep while she could.

"Rest, my dear, we're home," her husband said to her, softly. He knew just the words to comfort her. She managed a grin for him before she closed her eyes. How she loved her husband and this new land, its produce, the scenery, the springs and the rivers..."Oh, Papa, if only you could see us now!"

Hoglah was not tired, though she should have been. Like her mother before her, she had made this journey heavily pregnant and with several little ones in tow. The experience gave her new insight into how much her mother must have suffered and she was grateful that at least, when this new baby was born, there would be no shortage of water and a comfortable place to lie.

Hoglah, children sound asleep, took a moment to go outside and watch the moon rise over the mountains. Tonight it was pink, not shining silver, "Maybe it's a sign," she thought, "I will have yet another girl." She knew her husband would not dare say it, but was hoping this fourth child would be a boy. "Come what may," she whispered to herself, "God will provide!"

The whisper was heard. Her husband lay down the sword he was polishing, came up to her and slipped his arm around her waist.

"You know, whatever He provides, it will be our heart's delight!"

Hoglah's joy was complete. She leaned back into his shoulder, feasting on the Lord's goodness, a deep content washing over her soul.

Milcah felt like a queen. Here she was—at last inside brick walls. She placed her mother's lamp on a makeshift table and made herself a drink. She was settling down to married life now, although sometimes she still missed hearing Hoglah's morning songs and Tirzah's constant shrieks of laughter. Her young husband had found a small vacant cottage, right inside their allocated land.

"This will save us a lot of work, Milcah," he had said, quite pleased at securing such a prize, "And we can get on with planting some vines and maybe a fig tree to sit under."

Milcah, ever the queen, was quite happy with his suggestion, as long as she could be reasonably near her sisters. She was content, for now, to sit back and enjoy an easier life and share her husband's dreams.

The journey had been long, but, goodness, what incredible things the daughters had seen and done. Soon the eldest four were sound asleep, but Tirzah, true to form, was not tired and still very much excited.

"I'm going out for another walk," she whispered to her

husband. "What about you?" But he was already asleep. She knew that enemy eyes might not be far away, but was not afraid to go out alone. This was a night to celebrate and she was not done yet. She started walking, then raced to the top of the hill to stand breathless, gazing at the stars.

"Oh, God!" she cried out, dancing around, hands high in the air, "This land is delightful, totally acceptable—Tirzah's land!"

We too, have land to possess, promised by the Lord. Some promises are general, applying to all, while some are specific words, perhaps prophetically spoken, and designer-made for us as individuals. There is almost always a time gap between the giving of the promise by the Lord and feeling the land under our feet. And that is a time when we must be patient and tenacious, and continue in hope—just like the daughters of Zelophehad.

Five Wise Virgins

Zelophehad's daughters were five wise virgins—watchful, alert and ready. When the opportunity arose, their lamps were trimmed and ready.

Ten young girls, the New Testament parable tells us, were waiting for the bridegroom to appear. They expected him to arrive earlier, but, for some reason, he was delayed. Five of the girls were wise enough to prepare for such an eventuality; they bought and brought along extra oil, carried in another vessel. The remaining five girls were not as forward thinking—they did not stock up on oil, and their supplies ran out by the time the bridegroom called for them.

Lamps in those days were simple earthenware bowls, pinched in at the side to form a lip for the wick to sit in. Some lamps had two or more lips, allowing more wicks to be used, some were open and others partially covered. As the oil in the lamp burned off, the wick was left charred, causing the flame to smoke and the light to dim. For their lamps to shine brightly, the women had to trim their wicks, removing the redundant polluting part, and then refill the oil well. (See Matthew 25.)

There is an art to trimming a wick. If the job is rushed and it is cut straight across, the wick will be flat, and although it will work, the wick will not give the best light. Pointed trimming, in which the wick is carefully cut to a point, produces the brightest light. It takes more patience and time. Refilling with oil is another thing that takes time. To do this you have to go and collect it and pay the going rate for it.

The five foolish virgins were unprepared. They had not made the effort or paid the extra price to ensure a plentiful supply. These girls speak of those who know the Word of God, but who do not have the oil, the anointing of the Holy Spirit, to make them burn and shine. They have not planned properly, and yet when things come crashing down on them, they want others to make it easy for them.

All ten girls had a lamp, but half lacked the substance that brought illumination. A lamp without oil is of only decorative use. Only five girls carried their lamps with wisdom. The word *wise* used in this parable is *phronimos*, meaning "correct perceptions" or "good understanding."

Jesus knew about making the effort and paying the price. Gethsemane was a place of hard pressing; He was about to pay an enormous price on behalf of mankind, and when He most needed them, His friends deserted him. It was a place of being alone and surrendering to the will of God. What does this have to do with oil? *Gethsemane* means "oil press."

> Your word is a lamp to my feet and a light to my path.
> —PSALM 119:105, NKJV

The daughters of Zelophehad were a wise five. The wicks

of their hearts were trimmed in the desert season, and they had a good enough understanding of God's justice to be prepared, if necessary, to step into their Gethsemane—because that was where the richest oil was to be found.

Ranks of Five

It is significant that there were *five* daughters of Zelophehad. In Hebrew each number bears a meaning: five, *chamesh*, is linked to the word *chamush*, meaning "armed" or "with ammunition." This word appears in the Exodus story.

> So God led the people around by way of the wilderness of the Red Sea. And the children of Israel went up in orderly ranks out of the land of Egypt.
> —Exodus 13:18, NKJV, emphasis added

The phrase *orderly ranks* is *chamush*, sometimes translated as "in battle array." The people were led out of Egypt in military ranks of five, armed and equipped for battle. At the end of the desert period, not only did these five women move together, but the people moving into the land did so in ranks of five. (See Joshua 1:14.)

In 1 Chronicles 12:23, when the battle was on to make David king, it took men who could "keep rank" and were of "one heart." In the New Testament, a small boy came to listen to Jesus "armed" with five loaves of bread. As Jesus demonstrated the miracle of multiplication, He sat the five thousand in ranks of fifties and hundreds. Everything was done in an orderly way—ensuring no one could later suggest that only a few of the people had actually been fed.

And the church is effectively armed when the fivefold ministries of apostle, prophet, teacher, pastor and evangelist are marching out together, paving the way for others to follow.

Five of you shall chase a hundred, and a hundred of
you shall put ten thousand to flight: your enemies
shall fall by the sword before you.
—LEVITICUS 26:8, NKJV

Imagine what a city full of people moving in godly ranks
could do?

HOW MANY DOES IT TAKE?

But even without a team of five, we can still receive our
inheritance. Philip's daughters enjoyed an inheritance of a
rich prophetic gifting: four wise virgins. Five, four, what
about three? Yes, there is an inheritance account here, too.
Three sisters received an inheritance, in spite of having
brothers:

In all the land were found no women so beautiful as
the daughters of Job; and their father gave them an
inheritance among their brothers.
—JOB 42:15, NKJV

For added emphasis, the daughters, not the sons, are
named: Jemima, Keziah and Keren-happuch, and their
name meanings all speak of their beauty...but that's
another story.

Two sisters, Rachel and Leah, asked for an inheritance
from their father, Laban, and received it.

And then, to inspire those who do not have siblings, one
lone and remarkable daughter, Achsah, a contemporary of
the daughters of Zelophehad, boldly asked for an inheritance—a very special parcel of land.

CHAPTER 12

Passing on the Inheritance

*I pray also that the eyes of your heart may be
enlightened in order that you may know the hope
to which he has called you, the riches of his glorious inheritance in the saints.*
—EPHESIANS 1:18, NIV

N ow that Zelophehad's daughters were well known,
people often wanted their advice on issues, and their
diaries were always full. One day Tirzah arrived home from
being out with her husband and found a young girl waiting.
She was dressed in fine linen and wore several golden anklets
around her feet. It was Achsah, of the tribe of Judah, Caleb's
teenage daughter. Achsah had that same spunky fire as her
father, whose name means "the dog." His name suited him
because he had a dogged determination, and there was no
denying Achsah was his daughter. She was also his only
daughter, and she enjoyed the company of the daughters of
Zelophehad and being part of their sisterhood. She especially
liked Tirzah who had a similar youthfulness.

"What's one more Achsah?" Tirzah had offered years before.
"Join in the fun anytime; we'll adopt you as sister number six!"

Achsah enjoyed the fun and their humor, but more than

that, she was taken with the idea of women owning their own land.

On this particular day, Tirzah took one look at the girl's face, and she knew something was wrong. "What's happened?"

Achsah had traveled a long way to visit and was exhausted, but it was more than that. Tirzah suspected it might be something to do with Caleb. At eighty-five years of age, the man was still looking for new mountains to climb and new giants to conquer. On this side of the Jordan, war was almost constant, and Caleb was often up front beside Joshua, causing great concern for Achsah. But Tirzah was wrong; her father was not her worry this time, though he was indeed involved.

"I have been promised in marriage." The girl's face was tense as she blurted it out.

"Marriage!" Tirzah exclaimed, "but isn't that wonderful? Who is the lucky fellow?"

"That's the trouble, Tirzah," Achsah burst into tears and fell into Tirzah's arms, "I don't know!"

It turned out that Caleb, just back from three major battles to secure Judah, wanted help with a fourth. He had offered his daughter's hand to the man who had attacked and captured a portion of Judah, known as the City of the Book, or Kiriath Sepher. It was a place of great learning, a bastion of ungodly intellectualism and not about to fall easily.

Achsah sat down on the mat with her friend and sobbed her heart out. Tirzah listened patiently until the girl's emotions calmed.

"Achsah, you know what is certain?" The young girl did not look up. She sat crossed-legged on the floor, playing with the bells on her anklet. Tirzah smiled, knowing the girl's name meant "tinkling anklet." In fact, she had never seen Achsah without one, and everywhere the girl went, her presence was announced by the sound of tiny bells.

"You will end up marrying a mighty warrior, one strong in battle, well able to provide for your children in years to come. No," she went further, "not only strong, the strongest."

"Oh yeah?" Achsah retorted. "And who is the strongest, then—apart from my dad?"

The words Tirzah had uttered out of prophetic impulse, "the strongest," suddenly dawned on them both, and they spoke his name together.

"Othniel! It's Othniel!" Without doubt, he was the most outstanding warrior in the nation. Caleb's younger brother. Achsah's uncle.

"Oh, Achsah, Othniel is a God-fearing man, a good man, a true lion of Judah." Tirzah lifted the girl's chin so that their eyes met. "One day he will be a mighty leader, just like your father. You wait and see!"

"Yes, and just like my father, he is old!" Achsah shook her head, and once more tears welled in her large brown eyes. Othniel was not as old as his famous brother; indeed, he was a good bit younger, but in the eyes of a dramatic teenager, he was ancient.

"Uncle Lion," she wept, "I never dreamed I would be marrying him!"

Achsah stayed with Tirzah for a few days. Most of the time they sat quietly stringing necklaces, a welcome break from the constant talk of war outside. Of course they discussed other possible and preferred suitors, but mostly they talked about Othniel and Achsah's anxiety about having him as a husband.

On the morning she was about to return home, Achsah turned to her friend and said, "Tirzah, ever since I have known you, all I have dreamed of is having my own land. A nice place like yours, with plenty water. If Othniel wins, then I must live in the barren Negev with him."

Tirzah took the girl by the arm and squeezed firmly.

"Achsah, my sister, don't stop dreaming your dreams." Tirzah's eyes misted as she quoted her father, "Dream big dreams, child, dream big dreams."

And so it happened. Othniel, the lion of Judah, won the battle and secured Achsah, the anklet girl, as his prize. They had a huge wedding; Caleb spared nothing for his precious daughter, and the celebrations lasted for days.

Achsah was showered with gifts—including a golden anklet with the prettiest tinkling bells she had ever heard. When, late in the evening, she was invited to perform the bridal dance of Mahanaim, she took everyone's breath away. Bells ringing from wrists as well as ankles, her long hair flowing, she gracefully swept her way around the blazing campfire, in keeping with tradition, the sword in her hand raised to the sky.

During the feasts, Achsah overheard the men talking about the battles of recent days. They were also discussing a place with two splendid springs, one issuing from the higher part of the land and one from the lower. After a childhood in the desert, it sounded like heaven to Achsah's ears. She knew it was now or never.

That night she approached her new husband and put forward her proposal. His young wife's attitude pleased him, making him eager to satisfy her, and he approached Caleb early the next morning. Achsah waited, giving the men sufficient time to talk, and then saddled up and headed towards her father's camp.

Caleb helped Achsah dismount, smiling at her choice of transport—a humble donkey. "What is it you want, my daughter? Ask me and you will receive." Caleb had heard certain details from Othniel, but wanted to hear what his daughter had to say.

"Papa," she said, "The Negev is too dry for me. I've had enough desert. Anyway, didn't the Lord promise us a well-watered garden?" She paused, knowing how her father loved her, and plunged into her request. "Papa, I need a place with more life, with more water. I want the Springs." And then, quickly, remembering Tirzah's advice on manners and respect, "Uh, I mean, please, Papa, is there any way you can arrange for me to own the Springs?"

Caleb chortled to himself. Marriage had not changed his daughter. She was still as bold as ever, not only in asking for land in the first place, but also requesting the best there was. In addition she was asking for a double portion; both top and bottom springs. This vivacious girl brought such joy to Caleb, and her newfound courtesy, often forgotten in her enthusiasm, delighted his heart.

"Have you been visiting that Tirzah girl again?" Achsah grinned and nodded. Caleb smiled approvingly and granted her request. (See Joshua 15:17–19.)

OUR INHERITANCE

Achsah received because she dared to ask for what had been promised in her desert season. This astute young woman took possession of life-giving springs because she had a good relationship with her powerful dad. The daughters of Zelophehad received a solid inheritance because they knew the value of their father—and his name. As sons and daughters of the most powerful Father imaginable, we are also offered springs: an unlimited supply of life-giving water.

> For the LORD your God is bringing you into a good land, a land of brooks of water, of fountains and springs, that flow out of valleys and hills.
> —DEUTERONOMY 8:7, NKJV

God's springs have upper and lower reaches, just like Achsah's. The upper portion is our vast inheritance in Christ, which we will only fully comprehend when we go to heaven.

> For God has reserved a priceless inheritance for his children. It is kept in heaven for you, pure and undefiled, beyond reach of change and decay.
> —1 PETER 1:4, NLT

For now, on this side of eternity, we live at the lower springs level. The lower spring is constantly fed by the upper. It is God's will for the blessings of heaven to pour into our lives; that is why Jesus told us to pray, "Thy kingdom come, thy will be done in earth *as it is in heaven*" (Matt. 6:10, KJV, emphasis added). It is not His will for people to be thirsty, dry and barren. His will is for His kingdom river to flow down from heaven to earth so we may drink and be completely satisfied. God specializes in hard situations, turning rock into pools and flint into fountains. (See Psalm 114:8.) He asks His people to trust in His strength so "when they walk through the Valley of Weeping, it will become a place of refreshing springs" (Ps. 84:6, NLT). And there is more, in Isaiah:

> I will open rivers in desolate heights, and fountains in the midst of the valleys; I will make the wilderness a pool of water, and the dry land springs of water.
> —ISAIAH 41:18, NKJV

> The LORD will…satisfy your soul in drought, and strengthen your bones; You shall be like a watered garden, and like a spring of water, whose waters do not fail.
> —ISAIAH 58:11, NKJV

In desert seasons our spirits may feel parched as we walk through arid land with dried-up springs and waterless riverbeds. The flow of water may have been suppressed because of sin on our part, or because God, in His sovereignty, is testing our faithfulness. But when God blocks streams, it is with a purpose: to increase our capacity to hold more living water and enjoy more of His benefits.

> And though the Lord gives you the bread of adversity and the water of affliction…Then He will give the rain for your seed…There will be on every high mountain and on every high hill rivers and streams of waters…
> —ISAIAH 30: 20, 23, 25, NKJV

> Whoever drinks of the water that I shall give him will never thirst. But the water that I shall give him will

become in him a fountain of water springing up into everlasting life.

—JOHN 4:14, NKJV

After the season of discipline, refining or testing is over, heaven's floodgates reopen, and God's living water nourishes our lives, producing growth and fruit that would have been impossible before.

There is more to our birthright, however, than refreshing water to sustain our Christian lives and growth. Swimming in God's river brings refreshment, healing and restoration, but if we focus only on God's power, we have missed our main inheritance—God Himself. That's why David sang, "All my springs are in you," (Ps. 87:7) and "My flesh and my heart may fail, but God is the strength of my heart and my portion forever" (Ps. 73:26).

PRIESTLY INHERITANCE

The Levites understood this; they did not receive land—God was to be their "lot" in life. Some priests were named Hilkiah, which means "Jehovah is my portion." One such priest made a significant impact on society. This *Hilkiah*, a high priest and ancestor of Ezra, was cleansing the temple of idols when he found a major part of his spiritual inheritance.

Then Hilkiah the high priest said to Shaphan the scribe, "I have found the Book of the Law in the house of the LORD."

—2 KINGS 22:8, NKJV

A chain of events was set into motion: the priest passed the book of the law to his secretary, who passed it to the King, who in turn sought advice from his wardrobe master's unusual family. This family stitched and pressed more than designer clothing—they were skilled in prophesying God's designs. Their best-known prophet was Jeremiah, but King

Josiah turned instead to Huldah, Jeremiah's aunt through marriage. Jeremiah's prophecies were not easy on the ears. If Josiah thought he would get a softer word for his nation from a woman, he was wrong. Huldah was a strong prophetess who delivered a hard word. But, for Josiah personally, Huldah had some words of encouragement.

> Because your heart was tender, and you humbled yourself before the LORD... your eyes shall not see all the calamity which I will bring on this place.
> —2 KINGS 22:19–20, NKJV

Huldah's prophetic declaration led to the circle of influence being enlarged wider still. The king read the law to everyone—prophets, priests and people, "great and small." King Josiah was not interested in reading for head knowledge only: he covenanted to obey God and introduced substantial national and spiritual reforms, removing the idols, shrines and mediums and reintroducing the Passover.

All this because Hilkiah rolled up his sleeves, removed some idols, rediscovered his inheritance was God and passed that revelation on.

GOD'S LEGAL MATTERS

As most parents know, when you want to pass on an inheritance there is legal work to be done first—writing wills and testaments, sorting out title deeds, finding guarantors. God's legal matters are all taken care of, not by any old lawyer, but by the Supreme Judge—God Himself. His will and testament are written down in the Old and New Testaments. In Hebrews He outlines the conditions attached to any will.

> In the case of a will, it is necessary to prove the death of the one who made it, because a will is in force only when somebody has died; it never takes effect while the one who made it is living.
> —HEBREWS 9:16–17, NIV

Of course, the specific reference is to His Son. And Jesus' death enabled God's will to be put into effect. In Jesus we have not only a will, but also a covenant—an agreement between two living parties—and this one is a blood covenant.

> And He said to them, "This is My blood of the new covenant, which is shed for many."
> —MARK 14:24

Jesus was anticipating his imminent death on the cross. How can the cross, a tool of death, be an agreement between living parties? That problem was solved through the resurrection. Jesus, victorious over sin and death, now offers the covenant of life to anyone who goes to the cross and meets him there.

There is one more step to finalize the legal matters. Once the will is read and the covenant agreed upon, we receive legal documents, or title deeds, that substantiate ownership.

> Now faith is the substance of things hoped for, the evidence of things not seen.
> —HEBREWS 11:1, NKJV, EMPHASIS ADDED

The Greek word for substance here, *hupostasis*, can also be translated "title deeds." This title deed is not empty hope. It has substance, giving us an inheritance document that is signed with the blood of Jesus and stamped by the guarantor, the Holy Spirit, who sets a firm seal on the title deeds for us. (See Ephesians 1:1–14.) So God looked after the legal matters for us. All we have to do is "sign" the title deeds— our signature being faith in Christ.

Even when we have signed the title deeds by faith, and our names appear in the Lamb's Book of Life, the legal battles are not quite over: there are those ready to contest our rights, to stamp out our faith and steal the title deeds from us. Battle is never far away.

GOD'S WILL IS CONTESTED

Jephthah, from the same Gileadite clan as the daughters of Zelophehad, faced this problem a few generations after the women died. (See Judges 11.) He was a mighty warrior, as many of his descendants had been, but also the son of a prostitute. It was this and probably jealousy that caused his half-brothers to write him out of the family will.

> So Jephthah fled from his brothers and lived in the land of Tob; and worthless fellows gathered themselves about Jephthah, and they went out with him.
> —JUDGES 11:3, NASB

Jephthah retained the mark of a leader in spite of the pressures. But for a time, as it would be with David when he too faced rejection, the only people who seemed to want to hang out with him were rejects and rebels. Together they went on raids against their enemies, rather like Robin Hood and his band of merry men. News of Jephthah's victories spread and eventually the brothers had to eat humble pie. Jephthah was back in favor and was promoted to commander and judge of Israel.

When we face those who remind us of our past or are jealous of us and want take away our title deeds, we should do what Jephthah did—just get on with the adventure.

Jephthah's demonstration of power in battle testified to his relationship with God. And so it is with Jesus:

> For the works which the Father has given Me to accomplish, the very works that I do, bear witness of Me, that the Father has sent Me.
> —JOHN 5:36, NASB

We use the words *testify* and *testimony* so much, we can forget they bear a legal connotation. What Jesus did proved He was who He claimed to be. We are invited to do "greater works than these," verifying that His Testament is true. It is hard to imagine what greater work we can do than Jesus did, but whatever is meant, as we move out to love as Jesus loved, we will certainly face a battle.

SATAN CONTESTS GOD'S WILL

Satan will always contest God's will. He's lost his inheritance, and he hates to see others gain theirs. He will steal and destroy our destinies, if we let him. The Bible tells us to resist him, to hold up our shield of faith, and he will flee.

Satan includes lying in his battle strategies. We challenge God's will ourselves when we believe Satan's lies that He does not care, does not have a plan for our lives or will not provide all we need to accomplish it. When we lack faith in what the Lord says He will do, we are contesting His will.

Instead of being worn down in these skirmishes, self-inflicted or otherwise, we should hold our signed, sealed and delivered title deeds to a rich inheritance firmly in our hands and make sure we stick close to the Lord.

> The man who makes me his refuge will inherit the land and possess my holy mountain.
> —ISAIAH 57:13, NIV

Achsah knew about battling to take the land. She got off to a good start because she had a powerful and well-known father who modeled the best warfare principles. And in marrying the lion-man of Judah, her father's right-hand man, she always had a mighty warrior by her side protecting her.

Things changed. The people of Israel did not make God their refuge; instead they reverted to false gods. This led to eight years of suffering at enemy hands. But enough people held true; intercession turned the situation around, and the Lord appointed the first judge of Israel to lead the people back to godliness. Who did He choose? Achsah's husband, Othniel. Achsah, the anklet girl, became the First Lady of the land. Like the proverbial woman, she "considered a field"—a good one at that—"secured" it, then saw her husband "sit in the city gates" for the next forty years. (See Judges 3:7–11; Proverbs 31.)

Like Achsah, we have the Father's right-hand man by our side, Jesus the Judge of all, ready to protect us in the battles of life. When our world changes around us, and evil and godlessness seems everywhere, God will always be looking for those who are wise and courageous enough to choose the best inheritance and fight to retain it. These people, like Achsah and Othniel, will go places in God.

THE FATHER'S INHERITANCE

Our inheritance is one side of a coin. God the Father has an inheritance too, for His Son: people. (See Deuteronomy 32:9; Ephesians 1:18.)

The Father longs for the nations—every tongue and tribe—to present them to His Son. And since we share in the Son's inheritance, the nations are our inheritance, too. Referring prophetically to Jesus, David sings what is on the Father's heart:

> Ask of Me, and I will surely give the nations as Thine inheritance, and the very ends of the earth as Thy possession.
>
> —PSALM 2:8, NASB

> Go therefore and make disciples of all the nations, baptizing them in the name of the Father and of the Son and of the Holy Spirit, teaching them to observe all that I have commanded you; and lo, I am with you always, even to the end of the age.
>
> —MATTHEW 28:19–20, NKJV

Jesus' last words recorded by Matthew gave us instructions: we must go into the world with the message of our wonderful inheritance and our magnificent God. As we do, we will increase Jesus' inheritance, enlarging His kingdom, one by one, until the nations are back in the arms of God. When we focus on His inheritance rather than our own, we move from our deserts to our destinies. Paul knew the importance of having our eyes properly focused when he prayed for the Ephesians.

> I pray also that the eyes of your heart may be enlightened in order that you may know the hope to which he has called you, the riches of his glorious inheritance in the saints and his incomparably great power for us who believe.
> —EPHESIANS 1:18, NIV

The daughters of Zelophehad had hope-filled eyes. Five young virgins, lamps brimming with oil and wicks well trimmed, asked for their inheritance and received it. In doing so they also left a mark in Jewish society. But could they have imagined, in their wildest dreams, how much further their influence would reach?

ANOTHER WISE VIRGIN

It had been yet another day of visitors. The astronomers had seemed wise and knowledgeable about many matters. They, like the shepherds who had called in a few months before them, had known the child was special. When they saw him, they immediately knelt down, ornate silken robes flowing. Each offered a gift, strange choices for a baby, but each worth more than Mary and Joseph could fathom. Mary, pondering the meaning of the gifts in her heart, opened the only large storage box they owned and lowered in the items, hoping that some, like the burial myrrh, would not be needed for a long time.

After singing reverently in their own language, they politely asked the young mother if they could hold her infant. They wept, as if lost for a moment in another world, while little Jesus looked up into each face with sparkling eyes and smiled a perfect little baby smile. There was a holy hush in the room, undisturbed by the noise of the crowds milling outside.

Mary had offered simple refreshments to the guests, while Joseph went outside to ensure their servants and camels, a large entourage, were not in want. In Joseph's absence, prolonged by inquisitive townsfolk, the conversation took an unusual turn. For foreigners, the wise men knew much about Jewish history, more than Mary knew herself, and they also knew a great deal about Jewish law.

It was evening before Mary and Joseph were finally alone with their child. Tired, but in good spirits, they sat down to relax.

Mary rocked her baby in her arms and smiled at Joseph. "He is such a peaceful baby, isn't he?"

"Prince of Peace," chuckled Joseph, stroking the child's rosy cheeks.

"A Prince, from the royal house of David," Mary added, her tone and the glint in her eye beckoning a response from her husband.

Before they were betrothed, the couple had enjoyed teasing each other over their family lines, but when the baby arrived, the banter, no longer amusing, stopped. Each was a descendant of the great king, but it appeared neither could pass on the blessings.

Joseph knew the child was not of his own seed, but loved the boy as if he was his own and gave him full adoption rights. Full rights, however, meant passing on the curse of his lineage—"no good thing" would come out of the house of Jeconiah. Joseph looked at the sleeping babe thinking, "This one doesn't deserve to bear such a heavy heritage." Curse or not, Joseph would give the child his name and write his name into the family records. Little did Joseph know, the infant would bear a far weightier curse than Jeconiah's.

Joseph thought back to the last time they talked of their roots. Lineage had been the "in" topic; Caesar had called a worldwide census, requiring people to return to their ancestral towns. For Joseph, that was this royal town of Bethlehem. No sooner had Joseph entered his name in the Roman books, when Mary had felt her first contraction. Joseph collected his thoughts and came back to the present, setting his gaze on the child. The precious baby was here, right here.

"Ah, Mary, it's a sad thing that I cannot give the child royal blood without a curse."

Mary straightened in her chair. It was time to tell Joseph what the men had told her.

"He has royal blood without the curse," she said, "from my side of the family!"

"But Mary, my love," Joseph responded hesitantly, wondering how she could be saying such a thing, "that line died with your father, surely."

Mary had waited for this moment since the visitors and crowds had left. In spite of her tiredness, her heart raced with excitement. Now, at last, with no other listening ears, she could tell him.

"That's true," Mary replied, "my father died without leaving any sons. But, Joseph, I…I am a daughter of Zelophehad!" Mary looked at Joseph to see if he was grasping what she was saying, then continued. "As a woman without brothers, I can take my father's inheritance and pass it onto my son."

Joseph's face lit up. "Why, yes, of course!" he said, "I'd forgotten about them."

"Most people have, but without the daughters of Zelophehad, our son could not be truly from the royal line…" Mary winked at Joseph, "…without a curse!" Joseph beamed. "Just as well you married within your tribe then, sweet Mary, isn't it?"

OVERCOMING THE KINGLY CURSE

The Lord had made it clear in Old Testament times that the

Messiah would be a king from the tribe of Judah and the line of David. Matthew's gospel records this Messianic line from Abraham to Joseph. Joseph, through his marriage to Mary, was considered the legal guardian of Jesus, but his family tree had a problem, a blood curse because of the wickedness of King Jeconiah.

> This is what the Lord says: "Record this man as if childless, a man who will not prosper in his lifetime, for none of his offspring will prosper, none will sit on the throne of David or rule anymore in Judah."
> —Jeremiah 22:30, NIV

If no one from Jeconiah's line could sit on the throne of David, how did Jesus manage to legally fulfill the prophecies that He would be King? The answer lies in Mary's line. Luke, as a good doctor, supplies us with a biological or human line in Jesus' genealogy all the way back to Adam. From Abraham to David, Mary and Joseph's family trees are the same, but then they branch off: Joseph's through Solomon and Mary's through Nathan, another son of David. Mary's genealogy ends with her husband's name, not her own, according to cultural practice at that time, but it was nonetheless the record of an uncursed kingly inheritance. The trouble was, women could not pass on an inheritance unless they fell into the same category as the daughters of Zelophehad.

C. I. Scofield states that Mary, like the daughters, did not have brothers, and so had a legal right to her father's kingly lineage, but only if she married within her tribe—and, as Joseph so quickly and rightly recalled, that is what she did.[1]

EPILOGUE

Leaving Footprints in the Sand

The daughters of Zelophehad would not have known the impact their lives were to have on our Savior's genealogy, so many years later, or that their names together read like a hidden redemptive plan:

Zelophehad: representing the shadow of death caused
    by sin
Mahlah: the weakness in Egypt
Noah: the wandering in the desert
Hoglah: dancing with joy as they feasted with the Lord
Milcah: the crossing over the Jordan into ruling and
    reigning
Tirzah: the total delight in God's eyes of the bride of
    Christ.[1]

What's in a name? A *lot* if you are a daughter of

Zelophehad. They inherited, so He could inherit, so we could inherit. As Mahlah, Noah, Hoglah, Milcah and Tirzah reached out for their father's inheritance, they stepped from the desert into their destinies. In taking that step, five ordinary young women left extraordinary footprints in the sand.

Notes

CHAPTER 1
Leaving Goshen

1. Adam Clarke, *Clarke's Commentary* (Nashville, TN: Abingdon, n.d.), s.v. "Goshen."
2. James Orr, ed., *International Standard Bible Encyclopedia*, s.v. "Rameses," http://www.searchgodsword.org/enc/isb/view.cgi?number=T7209.
3. M. G. Easton, *Illustrated Bible Dictionary*, Third Edition (Nashville, TN: Thomas Nelson, 1897), s.v. "Rameses."
4. Roswell D. Hitchcock, An Interpreting Dictionary of Scripture Proper Names, s.v. "Pithom," http://www.biblestudytools.net/Dictionaries/HitchcocsBibleNames/hbn.cgi?number=T2019>.
5. Ibid.
6. *Carriers of God's Glory*. Available from Master Potter Ministries, 3507 E. 107th Terrace, Kansas City, MO 64137.
7. *World English Bible*, Rainbow Missions, Inc., http://WorldEnglishBible.org.

CHAPTER 2
Zelophehad

1. Bruce Wilkinson, *The Prayer of Jabez* (Sisters, OR: Multnomah Publishers, 2000).
2. William Smith, *Smith's Bible Dictionary*, s.v. "Shiloh," http://www.biblestudytools.net/Dictionaries/SmithsBibleDictionary/smt.cgi?number=T3958>.
3. More information is available at http://www.christiannet.co.za/revival/mariaw.htm.

CHAPTER 3
Korah

1. Hitchcock, *An Interpreting Dictionary of Scripture Proper Names*, s.v. "Korah."

CHAPTER 4
Mahlah

1.More information is available at http://www.vbm -torah.org/archive/18/11selach.doc

CHAPTER 5
Noah

1. John Oxenham, "In Christ There Is No East or West." Public domain.
2. *Transformations II: The Glory Spreads*, video by TransformNations Media, a division of the Sentinels Group, WA.

CHAPTER 6
Hoglah

1. Francis Brown, S.R. Driver and Charles A. Briggs, eds., *A Hebrew and English Lexicon of the Old Testament* (Peabody, MA: Hendrickson Publishers, 1979).
2. Smith, *Smith's Bible Dictionary*, s.v. "partridge."
3. Easton, *Illustrated Bible Dictionary*, s.v. "partridge."
4. Charles Wesley, "And Can It Be That I Should Gain?" Public domain.
5. More information is available at http://www.rabbifinman.com/eparsha/matos maaseh5761.htm.
6. R. Thompson, *The Feasts of the Lord* (Medford, OR: Omega Publications, 1989).

Notes

Chapter 7
Milcah

1. For more information about Queen Amina,
    http://www.swagga.com/queen.htm, accessed June, 2003.
2. Queen Nandi and Nehanda, ibid.
3. For more information see
    http://www.geocities.com/Athens/Troy/1355, accessed
    June, 2003.
4. *Book of Christian Quotations* (Oxford: Lion Publishing plc,
    1997), page 196, section 19.156.2.
5. *Book of Christian Quotations,* page 95, section 16.23.1

Chapter 8
Tirzah

1. For more information, see
    www.bible.org/cgibin/netbible.pl?book=sos&chapter=5,
    with reference to Ginsburg, Gordis and Deere.

Chapter 9
Character of a Daughter of Zelophehad

1. Scholars are unsure what the Urim and Thummin were. The
    view expressed here is one of many suggestions.

2. Adam Clarke, *Clarke's Commentary* (Nashville: Abingdon,
    n.d.), s.v. "Exodus 35:26." "In different parts of Asia
    Minor, Syria, Cilicia, and Phrygia, the goats have long,
    fine and beautiful hair, in some cases as fine as silk,
    which they shear at proper times, and manufacture into
    garments."

Chapter 10
Family Matters

1. Debra Evans, *Women of Courage* (Grand Rapids, MI:
    Zondervan, 1999).
2. For more information about Marcella and Paula, see
    http://www.geocities.com/karenrae.geo/marpaula.html,

accessed May, 2003 and
http://www.gospelcom.net/chi/DAILYF/2002/01/daily
-01-31-2002.shtml, accessed May, 2003.

3. Patricia Demers, *The World of Hannah More* (Lexington, KY:
University of Kentucky Press, 1996).

4. Walter Clark, Address by Chief Justice Walter Clark Before the
Federation of Women's Clubs, New Bern, N.C. May 8,
1913. Further information available at
http://docsouth.unc.edu/nc/clark13/clark13.html, accessed
September, 2003.

5. For more information about the Famous Five, see
http://collections.ic.gc.ca/famous5/achievements/
suffrage01/html, accessed May, 2003. For more information about Canadian women, see
http://www.nlc-bnc.ca/nl-news/1999/oct99e/3110
-15e.htm, accessed May, 2003, and National Library
News, October 1999, Vol. 31, no. 10, www.nlc
-bnc.ca/2/12/index-e.html, accessed May, 2003.

6. For more information about Razia Ismail Abbasi, see
http://www.worldywca.org/common_concern/june1999/.

CHAPTER 11
Taking the New Land

1. M. G. Easton, *Illustrated Bible Dictionary*, third edition
(Thomas Nelson, 1897), s.v. "Sharon." J. D. Douglas, ed.,
The New Bible Dictionary (Downers Grove, IL:
InterVarsity Press, 1975), s.v. "Sharon."

2. *Lion Handbook to the Bible* (New South Wales: Anzea
Publishers, 1979), s.v. "Joshua."

3. Douglas, *The New Bible Dictionary*.

4. For more information about Tirzah, see www.ourfatherlutheran
.net/biblehomelands/palestine/tirzah.htm, accessed May,
2003.

CHAPTER 12
Passing on the Inheritance

1. C. I. Scofield, *NIV Scofield Study Bible* (New York: Oxford University Press, 1967), 1054.

EPILOGUE
1. *Clarke's Commentary*, s.v. "Numbers 27."

TO CONTACT THE AUTHOR

If you have enjoyed this book, Wendy Yapp would love to hear from you.

Internet address:
www.wendyyapp.org
www.prayercare.org

Email address:
deserttodestiny@prayercare.org

Desert to Destiny guest book:
www.wendyyapp.org/desert2destiny/
guestbook.html

When you write, please feel free to include your testimony or help received when reading this book. Your prayer requests are welcome via our Web site, but please note, we may not be able to respond to each one personally.

PrayerCare International
P.O. Box 16
Karrinyup, WA 6921
AUSTRALIA